Critical acclaim for Olivia St. Claire

'Steamy but oh so discreet, *203 Ways to Drive a Man Wild in Bed* is *the* sensual guide to the way around a man's body'
New Woman

'A mind-boggling array of tips on how to spice up your love life'
Daily Express

'Olivia St. Claire covers every aspect of whacking up the intensity of your most intimate moments'
More

'Brighten up your love life . . . If you're short on ideas, buy Olivia St. Claire's *203 Ways to Drive a Man Wild in Bed*'
Cosmopolitan

Also by Olivia St. Claire

203 WAYS TO DRIVE A MAN WILD IN BED

227 WAYS TO UNLEASH THE SEX GODDESS IN EVERY WOMAN

and published by Bantam Books

302 ADVANCED TECHNIQUES FOR DRIVING A MAN WILD IN BED

Olivia St. Claire

BANTAM BOOKS

LONDON • NEW YORK • TORONTO • SYDNEY • AUCKLAND

302 ADVANCED TECHNIQUES FOR DRIVING
A MAN WILD IN BED
A BANTAM BOOK : 0 553 81473 7

Originally published in the United States by Harmony Books,
a division of Random House, Inc.
First publication in Great Britain

PRINTING HISTORY
Bantam edition published 2002

5 7 9 10 8 6 4

Design by Susan Maksuta

Set in 11.5/13 Cochin by
Falcon Oast Graphic Art Ltd.

Bantam Books are published by Transworld Publishers,
61–63 Uxbridge Road, London W5 5SA,
a division of The Random House Group Ltd,
in Australia by Random House Australia (Pty) Ltd,
20 Alfred Street, Milsons Point, Sydney, NSW 2061, Australia,
in New Zealand by Random House New Zealand Ltd,
18 Poland Road, Glenfield, Auckland 10, New Zealand
and in South Africa by Random House (Pty) Ltd, Isle of Houghton,
Corner Boundary Road & Carse O'Gowrie, Houghton, 2198, South Africa.

Printed and bound in Great Britain by
Cox & Wyman Ltd, Reading, Berkshire.

Papers used by Transworld Publishers are natural, recyclable products made from wood grown in sustainable forests. The manufacturing processes conform to the environmental regulations of the country of origin.

Acknowledgments

My deepest gratitude goes to all those who helped me give birth to this book, most especially: my editor, Shaye Areheart, who provided the kind of encouragement, guidance, and advocacy every author dreams about; my agent, Paula, who gave me the best kind of patient support and brilliant counsel throughout its long gestation period; my 'sister', Lorraine, who helped me remember what I'm really talking about; my dear friends Karen Marie, Claudia, and Deborah, who support and inspire me with their willingness to be wild and outrageous as well as deeply feminine; the Girls – Barbara, Kay, Ilene, and Toni – who help me stay connected to the spirit, variety, and crazy joy that is Woman; Barb, Chris, and Marianne, fellow adventuresses in the territory of love; and my beloved husband, the Sun in my universe, who every day inspires and excites me, teaches me the real meaning of love, and makes me feel like the Queen of his Heaven.

Acknowledgements

Contents

302 ADVANCED TECHNIQUES FOR DRIVING A MAN WILD IN BED

1

the love trance

Move into the love act so deeply that the actor is no more. While loving, become love; while caressing, become the caress; while kissing, be the kiss.

—*Lord Shiva*

Several years ago I had a sexual epiphany.

It was like when you learn to dance. You practice the steps and turns. You wear the right flowing dress. You get good enough to throw in a few hip wiggles and head tosses. You even teach your partner a few things. Then one day, some inner mechanism silently drops into place, Ginger Rogers possesses your body, and your feet don't touch the floor anymore. You're no longer a woman dancing the tango; now you're the tango dancing you.

That's how it was for me when, exhausted and culturally shocked after back-to-back trips to Japan and Egypt, I began a new love affair. In Japan, I had been a professional business-woman, promoting my new book, *227 Ways to Unleash the Sex Goddess in Every Woman.* Egypt, on the other hand, had been a personal spiritual pilgrimage. I had gone immediately from the confined spaces, techno-sex-kink, and cool, politely reserved people of the Orient to the vast, hot landscapes, pyramids, and fiery, demonstrative people of the Mideast. Little wonder, then, that on my return, when I found myself in the throes of a new romance, I was ripe for a spectacular fall on the dance floor or serious enlightenment.

Kirk was a sculptor who created huge works of red clay as voluptuous as they were impossible to interpret. As he worked, his long hair was always flying, his arms waving wildly, and his eyes glinting with artistic fire. Obviously, he had great hands.

We had had our first sex in his car, in a public park: under-the-steering-wheel, over-the-top-of-the-seat, the hot animal-lust kind. A few days later he invited me to his studio, where, suave and intense, he slowly removed one of my shoes and began rubbing the arch of my foot. 'I never drove with a woman in my lap before,' he cooed. 'It was sexy the way you totally surrendered, even your safety, to me.' Now sliding his sculptor's fingers up to my thigh, he looked me straight in the eye and whispered, 'You made love to my whole body, like a virtuoso playing an instrument. A virtuoso with hot flesh.' Caress, caress. Hot glance. Soft moan. 'You dug your fingernails into my back. I loved the scratch marks I found there the next day.' Deep ragged breath. 'You stunned me.'

I was pretty stunned myself. Intoxicated by the richness of the widely divergent cultures I had recently visited, Kirk's provocative words, and the racy idea of proud scratch marks, I was suddenly transported back to the wildness and abandon of that moment in the car. I could taste Kirk's desire as it mixed with the blood in my veins. And in the grip of some delicious oblivion, I felt myself slide across an invisible border, where I slipped on the role of love priestess like a new silk shirt. Suddenly I had access to a vast and ancient catalog of secret tricks. My bones simply knew what to do. Sex was dancing me.

Without a word, I went to the bed and threw the covers off onto the floor, as if clearing the altar for a sacred and outrageous rite. Undulating to some primal rhythm, I slowly stripped off my clothes, my hot eyes riveted to his. Finally I was left with only the long silk scarf I had been wearing around my neck. After trailing it over my breasts and hips, I passed it between my legs a few times to give it my own personal perfume. Suddenly I pounced on Kirk, ripped his shirt off, and tied his hands to the bed with my aromatic silk scarf. His eyes glowed with anticipation and just a hint of fear.

Possessed by passion, I licked the pale, tight skin on his stomach, his sinewy forearms, the hollow of his elbow. I bit his neck and scratched his chest, knowing he'd treasure those new marks. Then, like some hot and holy harlot, I stood on the bed over him and made him watch me pinch my breasts and massage the hidden well of my sex. He growled with lust. Bending down, I moved his briefs aside just enough so I could lick along the edge, in that sensitive place where inner thigh meets groin. I murmured softly, 'You're so hot here.' I felt his shaft, all scorching and alive, shiver next to my cheek. Now reeling with fever, I tore a hole in the constraining cotton of his shorts and lowered myself over him.

Afterward, I lay there, breathing in the pungent aroma of our sex, my heart pounding hard against the hot sheets, and smiling. I had surrendered to the rapturous swoon of loving. And like some ancient alchemical formula, that swoon had transmuted my everyday self into a modern-day Aphrodite. My heart and mind were open to the secrets of all the sex goddesses who had come before me and to the very spirit of sex itself. This, I knew, was the natural birthright of every woman. This, I knew, was a state as easy to fall into as an ocean wave, and as emboldening as a new pair of Manolo Blahniks.

All you need are the right triggers.

passion triggers

Whether it's a silk teddy, a succulent mango, or the memory of making love in the foamy surf, a Passion Trigger is something that connects you to your most primal, earthiest instincts. It breaks the seal of your everyday, mundane self and catapults you into delicious and wise abandon. Swept away by erotic impulses, you simply know how and when to apply just the right flick of tongue to an unawakened nipple. Steam radiates off your body, sending electric messages to his divining rod – and you become a true artiste of your own sexuality.

Such a prop or memory can cast its liberating and enlightening spell only if you allow it to. You have to deliberately surrender to its magic, letting texture, aroma, and fantasy work on your body. As it entices you into new worlds and exposes secret impulses, you have to dare to stretch the boundaries of your security zone, and to sink into the delicious dementia that is sex at its finest. In the words of D. H. Lawrence, you must be willing 'to risk your body and your blood and your mind, your known self and to become more and more the self you could never have known or expected.'

For example, you might pick up a black satin blindfold. You feel its silkiness, admire its soft curves, and sense its aura of mystery and forbidden pleasures. Your eyebrow seems to arch of its own accord, and instead of censoring yourself or succumbing to runaway prudence, you allow your mind to make a natural leap. What would it be like to blindfold your man? Your body remembers how the senses are heightened when sight is deprived, how you feel a little vulnerable, how exciting it is to switch roles. A warm tension begins to flow from your throat to your loins, your heart starts to flutter and your skin to tingle. You are in the grip of sensual, outrageous Aphrodite. Throwing caution to the wind, you sashay into your man's den, twirling the satin blindfold around your finger, a provocative look in your eye. Your erotic electricity crackles across the room, and he notices you, slightly dangerous and completely irresistible. Your work is already done.

Fortunately, almost anything can be the kind of catalyst that sweeps you away into full sex goddesshood. An ostrich feather, a fantasy, a French maid's costume, steamy language, Tantric art, or your man's pheromones can all be potent aphrodisiacs. As well as bringing heat to your loins and titillation to your imagination, they can invite the mysterious, the numinous, and even the gods and goddesses into your body.

See them, smell them, experience them as if for

the first time. Let your boundaries blur and your mind wander over all their wild and rapturous possibilities. Drink them in with *all* of your senses. Fantasize. Find out what about them makes you feel passionate, mesmerized, carried away by desire. Let the role of Naughty Lolita or Wanton Gypsy inhabit you. Sink into your lush, steamy self as into a hot bubble bath. These evocative Passion Triggers, and the glorious fog of sensuality in which they envelop you, can:

- make you *feel* sexy, at will
- safely liberate you from the grip of inhibitions, trepidations, and ironhanded Inner Prudes
- uncover hidden parts of yourself – deeper, wilder, more ancient and primal
- encourage you to travel just slightly over the edge of your usual sexual boundaries
- quicken your desire and adoration for your man's body
- inspire you to love your womanly body and become radiantly aware of its mystery and power
- transform simple technique into divinely inspired artistry

Notice there's nothing in this list that promises to give you Cindy Crawford's body, Cleopatra's proficiency, or Madonna's fearless audacity. That's because (and this has been confirmed by thousands of men) those things have so very little to do with being magnetically sexy. In the pages to come, I'll spell out lots of fun techniques and Passion Triggers to give you a jump-start, but it's the fire smoldering within you that will make them deadly.

2

the art of seduction

She spoke and loosened from her bosom the embroidered girdle of many colors into which all her allurements were fashioned. In it was love and in it desire and in it blandishing persuasion which steals the mind even from the wise.

—*Homer*

What makes a woman irresistibly charismatic? How does she become the kind of sexual sorceress who can put a man into a stupefied love trance just by touching his forearm? Even though every woman has the magical power to cause a man's sleeping snake to rise, why do some women seem to have it in spades?

The secret lies not in comeliness or technique but in the fearlessness to reveal your truest female self – a version of Woman unique only to you. Seduction is a natural result of knowing this womanly self so fully that you feel at home in your body – safe enough to experiment, play, and flower. When you understand that you are the only woman in the universe with your particular brand of feminine charm, you begin to appreciate your intrinsic value. You glow. Every gesture, word, and glance takes on an incandescent air of sensuality and charisma that the eyes of all mere mortals are drawn to.

Consider Marilyn Monroe, a pretty but insecure small-town girl who, unlike many other more beautiful women, became *the* sex goddess of our century. Or think of Cleopatra, not all that gorgeous and no more sexually astute than her many ladies-in-waiting, yet she enslaved the hearts of the two most powerful men of her time and became a sexual legend. Both Marilyn and Cleopatra knew who they were as women and *believed* themselves to be sex goddesses. As a result, their every move – and eventually their physical appearance – was imbued with an uncommon power that transcended eye-candy looks, the usual feminine wiles, and even the passage of time.

Every woman has her own unique brand of charisma, a personally 'embroidered girdle' of mental and physical allurements that trigger passion and erotic tingles for herself and all those around her. Find out which style of charismatic smolder most closely resembles yours and then, like the women given as examples, magnify it. Each of them has identified her own feminine currency and endowed it with a particular vibrancy, edge, and lushness. These women amuse and enchant even themselves. Like them, occasionally try dabbling in other styles, too – just for fun, just to be unpredictable, just to be all woman. You will find yourself developing a new power – causing irresistible feelings, turning heads, and lighting fires. Revel in it. Nurture it daily. Brandish it. Because a woman expertly carving up the world with her unique feminine weaponry is the most seductive creature known to man.

What Is Your Brand of Charismatic Smolder?

Kittenish (e.g., Marilyn Monroe, Kim Basinger, Britney Spears). Capitalize on your glowing, touchable skin and pouty lips. Wear soft cashmeres and silks in shades of pink, peach, and tawny beige. Read lots of romance novels and occasionally don a French maid's costume to bring out your inner coquette. Lower your head in that shy Princess Di way and smile sweetly as you pet and whisper to your man. Cultivate demureness and that innocent-but-yearns-to-be-ravished look.

Exotic (e.g., Cleopatra, Lucy Liu, Iman). Dramatize your vivid features. Wear bold colors, things that jangle, and musky perfumes. Take ritual baths, fill your boudoir with candles, walk like a belly dancer, and have several Tantric sexual positions up your sleeve. Spread your intensity around like frosting on the spice cake of life.

Elegant (e.g., Audrey Hepburn, Jackie Kennedy, Gwyneth Paltrow). Show off your fine bone structure. Wear classic, expensive-looking clothes, simple hairstyles, and flowing lingerie. Indulge in frequent Swedish massage and the deep contemplation of Georgia O'Keeffe paintings. Arch your long neck when offering it for his kiss, and glide your fingers over his skin as if admiring Corinthian leather upholstery. Exude refinement and a sense of rich luxury.

Sporty (e.g., Sandra Bullock, Katharine Hepburn, Anna Kournikova). Flaunt your athletic body and sinewy muscles. Wear perfectly fitted jeans and T-shirts or sporty spandex. Let the acrobatic possibilities of a 'love swing' or a whiff of your man's active pheromones ignite your erotic imagination. Make him laugh, challenge him to a game of strip billiards, and be gymnastic in bed. Radiate vibrant health and an irresistible joie de vivre.

Fiery (e.g., Tina Turner, Jennifer Lopez, Maureen O'Hara). Accent your eyes, which burn with an internal flame. Wear bold jewelry, slinky outfits that hug your figure or swirl around you, and lots of red. Shake your hips to hot music and go on spontaneous reconnaissance missions to sex-toy stores. Growl, pant, and claw like a tigress in the bedroom. Be so passionate about life that your inner fire sends sparks across any room.

Smart (e.g., Helen Hunt, Mira Sorvino, Sharon Stone). Don't be afraid to let intelligence and depth shine through your eyes. Dress with taste and style and wear the occasional quirky accent, something that has an interesting story behind it. Indulge in outlandish fantasies about the guy in front of you at the ATM, and develop a vast vocabulary of steamy language. Quote from the *Kama Sutra*. Introduce your man to a sensual piece of art or music, and tell him something fascinating about himself. Project mystery, depth, and worldliness.

Earthy (e.g., Sophia Loren, Janis Joplin, Jacqueline Bissett). Play up your voluptuous figure and womanly walk. Wear low-cut gowns, high heels or bare feet, and Merry Widows under tailored business suits. Lick food from your fingers, let wine drizzle down your chin and into your cleavage, and create a pleasure chest of fur mitts and ostrich feathers. Give your man plenty of smoldering glances and husky-voiced promises. Tease him with your hot touch. Be shamelessly lusty.

Wild Woman (e.g., Madonna, Mae West, Angelina Jolie). Wield your outrageousness like an electrifying weapon. Wear leather, over-the-top frills, garter belts, and wildly tousled hairdos. Have regular play dates with your flotilla of vibrators and make your own erotic videos. Make randy overtures in semipublic places, promise to tie him up, and bite his ear playfully. Ooze unpredictability, edginess, and a sense of delicious danger.

weaving a seductive web

When it comes to seduction, simple things make the most dramatic impact. If you add a touch of beauty, mystery, or danger to almost *any* situation or gesture, you will appear magical to him because you are unlocking worlds he otherwise doesn't know how to enter. Use your fiery, earthy, or elegant style of charismatic sorcery to make small shifts in his reality. You will find that, amazed and mesmerized by allurements he's never quite seen before, your man will come trailing happily after.

radiant beauty

Power attracts women; beauty attracts men. So find out what makes you *feel* beautiful, what turns on your inner glow. Because when you know and love who you really are, you will be more than beautiful. You will emit radiance – female sexual magnetism at its most potent.

1. The Native Americans regard women as the 'carriers of the seeds of beauty' (beauty meaning inner and outer aesthetics and harmony). Deliberately take on that mantle and be a source of beauty in his life. Always look and smell good. Accent your personal charismatic assets, and adorn yourself like a work of art. As they did in the ancient sexual healing temples, surround your man with beautiful and luxurious decorations – flowers, candlelight, heady aromas, music, velvety textures. Cook him sumptuous feasts to be eaten at romantic table settings. Point out the gorgeous sunsets that he's too busy or too muddled to notice. Read him the love sonnets of Pablo Neruda. Spin a web of beauty from which he will never want to escape.

2. Strew your bed with flower petals and roll around with him in their velvety, aromatic luxury.

Or float lots of rose petals on his bathwater and get in with him.

3. Outrageously flaunt the beauty of your erogenous zones. Wear peachy makeup and perfume on the nape of your neck, blush in your cleavage, red or sparkly rouge on your nipples, a thin gold chain around your waist, a lacy garter around one thigh, a sexy anklet, a silver ring and a pencilled-on beauty mark on one toe, or strawberry-flavored lipstick on the lips of your sex.

the tease

The promise of sex, and the challenge of getting it, will lure even the most invulnerable of men. Experiment with your eyes, words, and sense of style to find out what brand of tease complements your unique feminine nature and brings out just a hint of strumpet in you.

4. Eye contact can be deadly. When you're out in public, or meeting a man for the first time, hang on to his blinkers with yours as if glued to them. Nod your head ever-so-slightly and run your tongue over your lips, play with your hair, or roll your wineglass across the corner of your mouth, still maintaining smoldering eye contact. He'll be trembling with readiness, but simply smile demurely and start talking about the stock market,

slip off to the powder room, or plead another engagement and leave.

5. Gift-wrap a pair of lacy panties that you've worn all day and mail them to his office or hide them in his lunch box. Include a note that says, 'Thinking of you.'

6. *The Seven-day flirt.* Up-end the routine of an established relationship by taking seven days (or longer) to flirt madly with your man without having any naked contact or sex. Kiss passionately, dance together, run your fingers through his hair, prepare romantic dinners, caress his bottom as you walk by, maybe even flash him occasionally, but absolutely no sex. If he tries to initiate it, smile and tell him that if he waits just (however many) more nights, he'll get an extra-special treat. On the seventh night, with sexual tension at its zenith, pay it off with something exotic from chapter 9 or chapter 11.

7. Ignite his sexual imagination with one of Carole Lombard's little tricks (she was Clark Gable's main squeeze). Reportedly, the blond bombshell left a hand-knitted 'baton' warmer in Clark's dressing room with a card that said, 'Don't let it get cold. Bring it home hot for me.'

special touches

A man falls in love or lust with a woman, not because of how he feels about her, but because of how she makes him feel about *himself*. If you make him feel special, kingly, and powerful, he will be your helpless love slave.

8. *Praise.* Both in and out of bed, Cleopatra constantly lauded Caesar's wisdom, effectiveness, and godliness, telling him, 'The world, except for you, is filled with little men.' Find ways to make your man right during the day, and bolster his fragile male ego at night by praising his hardness, size, power, and the way he drives you crazy with lust.

9. *Erotic bonding.* Experiment until you find a simple, unique gesture that creates a special bond between the two of you. Whether it's the way you cradle his head in your lap and soothingly stroke his brow, scratch his back during the throes of his orgasm, or gently suckle his love organ until he falls asleep, every man has an emotional hot spot that makes him feel adored, manly, and profoundly safe. Once you discover it, he will yearn for your special loving without really knowing why.

10. *Love his body.* Treat his entire body like a delicious piece of candy you can't wait to suck

on. Drool over it. Find out what makes him breathe hard, and then focus your eyes and your attentions on that area until it's unbearably aroused. That territory is now yours. Determine the one thing about his body – rippling chest, grabbable butt, untiring love tool – that best lights your fire, and dote on it. He'll be seduced by your adoration, and you'll be irresistibly in lust with him.

posing

A seductress is proud of her body and knows that the mere sight of it can cast a bewitching spell on her man. Whether your best asset is a golden mane of hair, full creamy breasts, or an instep made for stilettos, highlight it, pose to show it off, let its power trigger your own primal instincts. In doing so, you are reclaiming the most ancient and powerful arts of your body.

11. ***Raising your arms.*** A seductive pose found in hundreds of ancient goddess statues, the elevation of a woman's arms signifies power and openness, to say nothing of the way it lifts and exposes your beautiful breasts. Just think of how many times you've seen that hand-behind-the-head pose in girlie magazines and calendars. It's coy and brazen at the same time. And if done with sensual deliberation, merely lifting an arm to arrange your hair, to rise up out of the bath, or to stretch like a cat can rivet your man's attention and make the air crackle with a female power surge.

12. *Opening your legs.* When you open your legs, you open your whole self, issuing your man the mysterious invitation he has craved since the beginning of time. You can send erotic sensations shimmering through both his and your limbs by performing this simplest and oldest of gestures. Focus all of your energy in your womb, think about how beautiful and juicy it is, and then, knowing it to be an act of immense power, slowly part your thighs. Offer him a view of your covered furrow while you're lazing around watching TV, give him an intoxicating glimpse as you get out of the car, or sit on the edge of the bed and spread your creamy thighs wide in complete mastery of both his and your libidos. It really is that simple.

13. *Hip swaying.* In many African cultures, a woman's hips are regarded as her most potent sexual weapon. Young girls are instructed in how to swing their hips as they walk to attract men, and how to circle them during sex to bring on their partner's orgasm. So don't simply clomp around from point A to point B. Undulate. Allow your natural womanly rhythm to move your hips and bottom in a mesmerizing sway that proclaims, 'I'm all woman!' Let your hips be loose and fluid when your man is pumping into you, creating the impression and the feel of orgiastic lust.

The Fine Art of Skirt-Lifting

An ancient gesture of female power, the uncovering of a creamy thigh, plump bottom, or dark, mysterious vee has been a staple of seduction for thousands of years. Aphrodite undraped her behind, Victorian ladies bared their ankles, French Follies dancers did the cancan, Monroe stood over a subway grating with skirt billowing, and female hitchhikers the world over raise their skirts to ensure getting a ride. If it's been working all these years, there must be something to it.

The Attitude

Never forget that what you have under your skirt is the Mystery of Mysteries, the Holy Grail that men dream about, scheme over, and sometimes lose their minds or fortunes trying to acquire. Your ultimate feminine power emanates like waves from the dark and dangerous cave between your legs. So tease, beckon, flaunt; reveal but conceal. Remember, you've got it; they want it.

The Skirt

The *best* skirt for lifting is: something filmy that reveals hints of the secret underneath; something tight that hugs, but not clenches, your curves; something short and flirty that could 'accidentally' bare more than intended; something long and billowy that flows with every step and hip sway; something with a thigh-high slit; or something spandex if you've got the figure for it. The *worst* is: anything long and baggy (comfortable but sexless); anything that would be considered 'business regulation' (boring); anything you can't walk in (how would you lift it?); anything too tight (crosses the trash threshold).

The Underpinnings

You want to uncover something that's really worth looking at, so your underwear is crucial. Wear lacy panties that look easy to rip off; a sexy garter belt and stockings; a beautiful thong; thigh-high, lace-topped stockings without panties; or absolutely nothing. On your feet, wear *high* heels or go barefoot. Do not under any circumstances wear tights, knee-highs, or Birkenstocks.

The Styles

The Hitchhiker: Scrunch up skirt on one side to reveal a thigh. Toe-pointing crucial.

The Sharon Stone Cross: Sensuously hike skirt on both sides, then sit with thighs very slightly parted. Cross, uncross, and recross your legs.

The Aphrodite Drop: Undrape one buttock from

the top. Glance over your shoulder to look at it, then at him. Or drop your skirt to the floor in one fell swoop.

The Cancan: Flash him with one quick, full raise – front or back.

The Madonna Power Hike: In *Body of Evidence*, Madonna's character stands atop a car hood, legs akimbo. She locks eyes with Willem Dafoe, slowly lifts her skirt to just above crotch level, raises her arms above her head, and silently dares him to come and get it.

Lolita: Wear a short skirt; bend over just enough to be naughty but still remain a lady.

The Gypsy: Raise your long, full skirt high on both thighs, but leave the middle draping down in front. Point one toe to the side, cock the other hip, look sultry.

The Monroe Butterfly: In a famous snapshot, Marilyn stands over a subway grating, high-heeled legs spread, and tries to hold her skirt down as the wind billows it up all around. If you can't arrange for a rogue breeze, twirl around to create a similar effect. Smile and look innocent.

The Subliminal Lift: Whisper to him what you are wearing, or not wearing, beneath your skirt, and he will mentally lift it for you.

14. *Posing like a goddess.* Many of the ancient statues of love goddesses show them posing in deliberately provocative ways. Inanna lifts her bare breasts with her hands, accentuating their ripe protuberance. The dakinis of India stand with one hand on their hip, the other resting in mock innocence atop their Great Jewel. Parvati sits with one heel pressed against her pubic mound and the other leg dangling gracefully off the edge of the divan. Designed to start sexual fever pulsing in their own as well as their consort's loins, these poses will lend you the power of the goddesses to charm, entice, and invoke sexual magic.

15. *Posing for the camera.* Take a snapshot of yourself dressed in revealing lingerie and/or posed in sexual invitation. Attach it to his shaving mirror, slip it into his book as a page marker, or cut it up like a jigsaw puzzle and mail it to him anonymously.

16. *Posing for the video camera.* Film yourself dancing around naked, doing a striptease, or pleasuring yourself to a steamy orgasm. Set him up in a comfy chair with a glass of wine and give him a private showing.

the smolder

17. Practice exhaling a sensual aura. It is said that the great Monroe generated an intense

sexual atmosphere because she thought about sex all the time, considering it with every man she met. Keep your sensuality close to the surface by fantasizing about your man, the gardener, the waiters at the Italian restaurant, and the Dallas Cowboys. No one but you will know. Wash dishes in the nude. Touch yourself sensually every day. Gaze at erotic pictures and imagine yourself into them. Don't wear any panties for an entire week. Think sex and your body will speak volumes.

18. When you're out for dinner, seduce him by helping to test the wine. Dip your finger into his glass and then, looking deeply into his eyes, smooth the grapey elixir over his lips.

19. As an elegant invitation to sex, cradle his hand in yours and kiss his palm lingeringly. Pause to glance up meaningfully. Then lick the soft hand pad and give it one delicate bite.

A Woman's Special Gifts

When we release ourselves from conventional thinking and self-criticism, our natural instincts begin to well up from within. Like the moon that rules our female natures, we become mediums for the eternal feminine – a condition mysterious and irresistible to most any man.

The Gift of Openness

Opening is a thrilling, and particularly feminine, act of seduction. Open your shirt. Open your legs. Open your eyes with invitation. Part your lips. Unfurl the petals of your heart. Lay bare your psyche to the wild and untamed. With your body, create an open receptacle to hold the mighty penetrator. This opening of self, as only a woman can do, is one of the simplest and purest techniques of ultimate seduction.

The Gift of Intuition

Whether or not you are highly intuitive, it's easy to create the stunning impression that you know what your man wants before he does. During a passionate kiss or embrace, imagine yourself melting into your lover and seeping underneath his skin. From there, you can more easily sense whether he is craving a hot lick on his neck, the feel of your nipples against his chest, or a ravishing pelvic thrust. Sometimes my man's ear looks completely irresistible and seems to be 'calling' to me. I lick it and he snuggles his ear against my lips. I try a little nibble. He shivers ecstatically, and I respond to his cue by slathering my tongue over his entire ear. As his whole body comes alive with pulsing urges, he marvels to himself at how well I know his secret desires.

The Gift of Surrender

In the same way you surrender to the beat and let the music dance you, or sink into the drowsy mood of a lazy afternoon, deliberately yield to the sensuality awakened by his touch. By submerging yourself in this swell of sensation, you trigger your passion. And a woman in full, undulating surrender to her primal passions is the most powerfully attractive magnet known to man.

The Gift of Dreams

When you touch a man's dreams, you seduce his heart. So as part of your bedtalk, ask your lover what he daydreams about, what his childhood fantasies were, and what kind of sex lives only in his imagination. Ask him to point out his favorite passages in *Penthouse Letters*. Invite him to create an outline for a book of adventure or a sex video starring the two of you. Several weeks later, pluck the strings of his heart by making his now-forgotten fantasy come true.

3

the games of love

Your professional name can be quite useful. Maybe you find it embarrassing to do sexy, outrageous things. But Mrs. X can do them.

—The courtesan to her student, in the movie
Sex and Mrs. X

Games, toys, costumes, and unusual places are marvelous tools for breaking down the barriers between you and abandoned, vixenish love-making. Don a slim skirt slit up to here, your tightest sweater, tottering heels, and Presto! Suddenly you look and feel like Brigitte the Bawdy Barmaid. Latch on to a vibrator and you are instantly atingle with the penetrating possibilities. And how can you help it if the spirit of competition in your strip backgammon match causes you to thrust his hand between your thighs?

Men thrive on variety, danger, and surprise. Let the powerful adrenaline and sheer kink of the new, the risky, and the unexpected sweep you away into a libidinous love trance that takes you both by storm.

location, location, and location

20. *Airport pickup.* When he returns from a business trip, pick him up at the airport dressed in a trench coat and heels. Escort him to a waiting limo, the kind that has a partition between the passengers and the driver. As you pour him a glass of bubbly, open your coat to reveal that you are wearing nothing beneath your businesslike wrap.

2 1 . *Hockey games.* Surprise him with tickets to a local sporting event. Bring a lap blanket and play with his hockey stick under cover while the crowd cheers.

2 2 . *Park bench delight.* After a night of dancing, my lover suggested a stroll in a nearby park. I led him to sit on a bench in a particularly dark corner. Lifting up my long, full skirt (under which I wore nothing), I crouched over his lap, opened his jeans, and mounted him. The darkness and my billowing dress kept our activities a thrilling 'secret.'

2 3 . *Shower goddess.* Surprise him by joining him in the shower, clad in a thin cotton slip or silky camisole. The wet, clingy fabric both looks and feels sinfully sexy.

2 4 . *Snowman.* On a winter hike or ski trip, drag him off into the forest and give him hot oral sex while he's braced against a tree. Apply a little snow for contrast. Or, like my brave friend Barb did, strip and have a shocking, hot-cold roll in the snow.

2 5 . *Locomotion.* Book a private train compartment and romance him with wine, exotic finger foods, and a boutonnière for his lapel. Then let the rocking, vibrating wheels underscore the wild rhythm of your lovemaking.

26. *Baseball field.* My friend Toni brazenly invited her first love out to the middle of a deserted baseball field one moonlit night. Prepared with blanket, picnic, and candles, she took him way past first base.

27. *Car wash.* Help him the next time he washes the car at home. Wear a thin white T-shirt, sit on the bonnet, and let water cascade over your breasts. Keep the hose streaming between his and your sweaty bodies as you straddle bumpers, boot lids, and bonnet mascots.

28. *Plastic room.* Cover the floor of a small room with a plastic tarp and spray it with whipped cream. Throw your man on top and get slippery with passion.

29. *Theater lobby.* Just before intermission at a play or concert, take your man out to the lobby and behind the vestibule doors. Pressed up against the wall, trousers and skirt at half-mast, you are in delicious danger of discovery – a position both desperately exciting and totally unforgettable.

30. *Waterplay.* Weightless, wet, and daring, sex in a tropical sea or wooded lake can provide the perfect touch of exotic adventure. Even just gliding his foreskin to and fro or pressing open the slit in his glans while it's beneath the

waves can create exotically slippery sensations. Float on your back and open your legs, inviting him to enter as you bob back and forth upon his rudder. Or simply hang yourself from his shoulders and hips and buoyantly bounce up and down. Swimming pools are inspirational, too. There, you can suspend yourself by grasping the lip of the pool and use it for leverage as he floats in from behind.

The Art of the Quickie

Making love in unusual circumstances often requires express-lane eroticism, so mastering the art of instant passion is essential.

- Start your heart pounding a few minutes *before* the event by imagining that swollen throb you feel when he licks your erect nipple.
- Once the quickie has begun, don't bother with clothes removal – no time, no need, no problem.
- To further heighten the fever, wrench yourself briefly away from him just before he penetrates you – breathe, smolder, anticipate, make him wonder. Then slam into each other like hungry animals.
- Your afterglow can be a loving kiss, a tender

caress, a soft 'I'm crazy for you,' or simply the hot sensation of having been ravished.

erotic games

31. *Hall of love.* Leave a trail of lighted votive candles through your bedroom, down the hall, or up the stairway. Be waiting for him nude on a sable bedspread, reclining in a soapy aromatic bath, or elegantly spread-eagled over the railing.

32. *Big spender.* Create an official-looking list of call-girl services and their prices. Present your man with a big wad of Monopoly money and tell him extras are available for big tippers.

33. *Treasure hunt.* One evening I left my laciest panties on the stairs, where I knew my lover would find them on his way in. At the top of the stairs lay some beribboned ostrich feathers, pointing meaningfully to the kitchen. From the kitchen doorway, he could see my black half-bra hanging on the refrigerator door, and inside the refrigerator he found a chilled bottle of champagne and fresh strawberries. On the same tray was a note challenging him to find a sex toy in the kitchen and bring all the items upstairs. Beginning at the top landing, I'd trailed some nipple tassels, a fishnet stocking, and a box of Kama Sutra Honey Dust all along the hallway leading to the master bedroom. There he finally

found me, togged out in a leather thong and five-inch stilettos, lying on a fur rug in front of a full-length mirror. The treasure hunt had ended, but the games had just begun.

34. *Strip pool.* For every ball sunk, the other person has to remove a piece of clothing. The winner can demand one sex act of choice before the next game. Decorate the cue sticks and table pockets with your discarded undies, and wear high heels so when you lean over for a shot, your bottom is nicely exposed.

35. *Porn star.* Watch an X-rated film together, then take on the roles of the characters in the steamiest scene and reenact it.

36. *Sexy Scrabble.* Follow the normal rules, but restrict yourselves only to words of hot passion and explicit sex. The one allowed exception is that, when adding on to existing words, you can make erotic phrases – for example, you can attach the word *me* to *lick,* or *naked* to *breast.* The other player must obey the written word.

37. *Hot-fudge sundae.* Cover your bed with a shower curtain and have him lie naked on top. Begin by drizzling warm chocolate on his toes, then licking each one with care. Encircle each nipple with whipped cream, top with a strawberry, and lay a stream of honey between all points. Smear his spoon handle with chocolate

sauce and coconut flakes. Dip chunks of banana in his chocolaty creaminess and feed him. Don't forget to smoosh some honey or chocolate on your breasts and mound, perhaps offering him a taste from the well of your desire. Then climb on and swivel.

38. *The Fantasy Game.* Keep a 'Fantasy Box' in the bedroom in which each of you can occasionally drop a note describing the kind of sex you dream about. Then some evening when wild inspiration strikes, take turns randomly selecting one of these fantasies to playfully act out, complete with costumes and props. Besides the taboo thrill and fun, these sexual imaginings can clue you in to his secret desire for, say, semipublic trysts (which you can surprise him with on another day) – and give him a subtle hint that perhaps you'd like more kissing and nipple-licking, whether it takes place on a fantasy fur rug or in your real-life bed.

naughty props

39. *Hanging chair.* I've never regretted one penny of the money I invested in my woven hanging chair. Nowadays you can buy a 'love swing' from any sex-toy catalog, adapt a small hammock, or simply suspend cloth strips from a branch, as people in the Orient have done for centuries. He stands, and you recline in the chair, suspended at waist level, legs gloriously splayed by

the supports. He can then swing you weightlessly back and forth upon his erection – quite an exhilarating feeling for both of you – and because there's so little effort involved, he can keep this up for hours. All hands are free to explore, and your G-spot is in for superb stimulation. For variety, he can sit in a regular chair, putting you, brazenly exposed, at mouth level. Or you can switch positions – you stand astride his swinging lance, or either of you kneel in the swing backward and rock. When he's in the suspended apparatus, add a touch of bondage by tying his hands to the supports above his head. Or get really brassy and transfer all of this to the children's swings in the park some dark night.

40. *Fizz ball.* Insert a moistened Alka-Seltzer tablet in your love tunnel and beckon your man to enter. Makes an invigorating fizzy tingle for both of you.

41. *Aromas.* According to a study by Alan R. Hirsch, M.D., director of the Smell and Taste Treatment and Research Foundation, a whiff of lavender increased the blood flow to men's organs by a whopping 40 percent. Vetiver, camphor, sandalwood, and ambergris are also purported to arouse and strengthen his member. Drop one or several of these scents into his bath, upon his pillow or bedside lightbulb, in his handkerchief, or on your nipples. Trigger your own love juices and fall into a reckless swoon by daubing on

jasmine, patchouli, or musk. Cleopatra didn't soak her sails in perfume for nothing! (By the way, in the above study, men's penises also became extra engorged when exposed to the smell of doughnuts, black licorice, and pumpkin pie. Start cooking!)

42. *Spreadables.* Anything that's edible and spreadable can be erotically applied. Try blue cheese dressing as a nice contrast to your coral opening; salsa to spice up his sausage; olive oil for glistening, lady-wrestler boobs; warm peanut butter and/or cold jelly on erect nipples; and sour cream atop his adorable bottom. The gastronomic possibilities are limited only by your imagination.

43. *Footstool.* So ordinary a prop, yet so divinely elevated an experience. Place a low footstool under your bottom, invite your lover to enter you in the missionary position, and rest your feet on his shoulders. He gets an exotic view and deep angle of penetration. You get intense G-spot stimulation. You can also assume the doggy pose atop the stool, allowing him to enter from behind in a near-standing position, where he can get extra thrusting power.

44. *Cardamom.* It is said that if you place this herb under your tongue and kiss your lover, he will be bound to you by invisible chains of desire.

45. *Armless rocking chair.* Obviously,

there are many delicious possibilities. But one I particularly favor is to straddle him as he sits in the chair, both your feet on the floor. Either of you can push with your feet to rock your hips, and all hands are available for body tweaking.

46. *Chocolate.* This food of the gods actually contains a substance that accumulates in the pleasure centers of the brain. Even just smelling it can intoxicate. Frost your shoulders, wrists, breasts, and open love lips with double dark chocolate icing (according to Karen Finley, star of *The Return of the Chocolate-Smeared Woman,* it's the most spreadable and besotting) and offer yourself for licking. Or erotically smear your guy with chocolate cream pie, slide against him, and lap up every drop. Don't forget the small of his back, a very erogenous zone for him.

47. *Daybed.* The armless ease of a daybed (you can also use two footstools, an armless reclining chair or sun lounger, or a suitcase with padding on top) provides the perfect stage for a provocative bump-and-grind. Have him lie atop the bed while you straddle the entire thing, then lower yourself onto his upright shaft. Your feet on the floor are the only support you need as you jiggle and thrust your unencumbered pelvis. Meanwhile, your hands can be undulating above your head, displaying your breasts, or flickering over his body. For variation, spin around, face his feet, and bounce your buttery bottom.

48. *Mask.* Wear a Mardi Gras mask to bed. It lends you mystery, dangerous beauty, and a licentious liberty.

49. *Lotions and powders.* There are many love oils, some pleasantly flavored, that actually heat the skin to produce delicious sensations when licked or blown upon. Heat Wave, Emotion Lotion, or Act of Love are thick enough to stay on the surface, building fire and desire, till sucked off. Outrageously decadent, Kama Sutra Honey Dust is 100 percent pure crushed honey – you dust it on with a feather, like powder, but it feels like a light oil. Powders, in fact, are great for adding slinkiness and decreasing friction. You can make your own inexpensive love powders by shaking cornstarch with vanilla, almond, or any other food flavoring you like. Trail, fluff, or flick any of these products across tender inner thighs, ticklish underarms, and erect appendages.

Going to the Movies

Film can provide great Passion Triggers. Aside from relishing any steamy sex scenes, be on the lookout for simple items and evocative images that you can use to unleash your uninhibited Inner Vamp, such as those in the following films:

Body Heat (Kathleen Turner's long, tight red skirt, slit thigh-high)

The Year of Living Dangerously (Sigourney's and Mel's rain-wet coats and hair)

Bull Durham (Susan Sarandon's toenail polish)

9½ Weeks (Mickey and Kim's strawberries at the refrigerator)

Dangerous Beauty (The sought-after courtesan's fur play mitt)

The Thomas Crown Affair (McQueen and Dunaway with the pieces of a chess set)

No Way Out (The backseat of a limo, Kevin Costner–style)

The English Patient (Ralph Fiennes, Kristin Scott Thomas, and a wall)

Basic Instinct (Sharon Stone's slicked-back hair, insolent gaze, and crossed legs)

All the Pretty Horses (Penelope Cruz's riding crop)

Quills (Kate Winslet's corseted bust, or Geoffrey Rush's enflaming books)

The Witches of Eastwick (How the devil made them do it)

The Fabulous Baker Boys (Michelle Pfeiffer's slinky red dress and a piano)

wicked wardrobing

Clothes can infuse you with sexiness and power. The right garment will make you move differently and provide you with the undercover freedom of another personality. Along with a plunging dress, pale angora sweater, or high-heeled boots, you also slip into a sultrier, softer, or more commanding version of yourself.

50. *Garter belt.* Pronounced the most exciting piece of clothing a woman can wear by 80 percent of men in a survey on sexual preferences, the garter belt is a lethal sexual weapon. Secretly wearing one under your business suit will make you walk differently – and *feel* more feminine and alluring; naughtier. Besides, parading around in front of your man with your thighs and bush exposed will drive him crazy with lust.

51. *Men's duds.* The contrast of your womanly body adorned only with his flannel or tuxedo shirt, the female version of Jockey shorts, or a man's hat and tie accentuates your feminine charms – and makes you feel more potent. Try a combo of his shirt and your thigh-high stockings.

52. *Matching underwear.* According to many call girls, men are especially aroused by flimsy bras and panties that *match.* It sends a

message: 'I'm hot. I know it. I flaunt it.' By the way, peach or pink shades make your skin look alive and ripe for touching.

53. *Corsets.* Custom-made lace-up corsets are the hottest trend in bedroom attire. They make you look and feel like a busty wench with questionable morals. In addition, the deliberate constraint forces your hot blood to all the right places and inflames your man with the desire to free you. I have a friend whose husband loves to watch her vacuum in her leather corset.

54. *Footwear.* Come to bed clad only in thigh-high vinyl boots, stilettos, ankle-strap high-heeled sandals, fancy cowboy boots, or anything made by Manolo Blahnik.

55. *G-string.* One woman told me, 'I behaved like a complete slut, but I was under the influence of my G-string and felt sexy.' No kidding! They make your love lips tingle and his mind focus. Combine a G-string with spike heels and a Wonderbra and you've got sexual dynamite.

56. *Merry Widow.* Some enchanted evening, emerge from the bathroom dressed in a sheer, beribboned Merry Widow (looking deadly and demure at the same time), saunter over to your google-eyed man, and kneel haughtily above his lips.

57. *Victoria's Secret model.* Buy a large trousseau of lingerie and tell your guy you need help in determining which things to keep and which to return. Light candles, put on 'Unforgettable' by Natalie and Nat King Cole, hand him a glass of wine, and model. Smooth your hands over your body a lot, move slowly, and smile. He'll gladly pay for everything.

The Art of Costuming

Costumes embolden us, evoke hidden personalities, and lend us the liberating power of disguise. My friend Kate dressed as a dominatrix for a Halloween party one year. 'I felt like a total sex goddess,' she says. 'I flaunted myself outrageously, 'whipped' everyone into a frenzy, and experienced feelings I didn't even know I had.' Meanwhile, men, who love variety, get the thrill of making love to 'another woman' while remaining faithful to you.

It doesn't have to be elaborate. Often, just one or two items will set the mood. With a short pleated skirt and pair of white knee socks, you can slip into the role of a kittenish Lolita, and invite your man to 'deflower' your virginal self. Put on your cowboy boots and red bandanna, and ride him like a pony. Submit him to your commanding sexual taskmistress by donning a military jacket or helmet.

Let your libido be your guide as you fantasize, explore, and select the appropriate attire for your every secret self:

- African princess
- Scarlett O'Hara
- French maid
- Greek goddess
- Zorro
- gangster's moll
- piratess
- Chinese dragon queen
- high-powered executive
- vampire
- geisha girl
- construction worker
- nurse
- leather fetishist
- policewoman
- Little Bo Peep
- proctologist
- Madonna
- Victorian schoolmarm
- la femme Nikita

dirty dancing

The combination of sexy clothes and undulating movement is almost too much for any man to bear. Using a long string of pearls, a feathered fan, or Gypsy Rose Lee's music as your Passion Trigger, let your Inner Exotic Dancer come out for a performance every now and then. If you're nervous, practice in front of a teddy bear first and imagine your man leering lustfully at you and praising all your moves. Or remember the priestesses of ancient Greece, who ceremonially danced around monolithic phalluses, their men in fear and awe of the power they generated. As the daughter-in-law of Pythagoras wisely said, 'A woman who goes to bed with a man ought to take off her modesty along with her petticoat.'

58. *Begin the beguine.* Setting the stage with Luther Vandross, candlelight, and champagne, invite your man to dance with you in the living room. Press yourself close, and glide your hands over his back and down to his rump. Softly rock your pelvis against his. Keep dancing while you slowly and deliberately remove your blouse, then his shirt, then your bra, rubbing your nipples across his bare chest. Continue stripping both of you, undulating against him, until his erection is unbearable.

59. *Gypsy fandango.* Layer on some voluminous long skirts and throw your wild inamorato to the floor. Stand astride him and wriggle, lifting your skirts so he can catch glimpses of your swaying jewel box, and occasionally stoop low enough for him to enjoy a brief touch or lick. A particularly racy addition to this dance is to apply rouge or red lipstick to your vaginal lips beforehand, perhaps even allowing him to watch you do this. Your outrageous behavior and beautiful self-decoration will present an unexpected and tantalizing challenge.

60. *Salome.* Light some musky incense, wrap yourself in lots of silk, sheer, or jangly belly-dance scarves, and perform the Dance of the Seven Veils. As you shimmy each scarf off, raise it overhead between outstretched arms, slide it over your face, breasts, and hips, pull it between your thighs, and toss it over your sultan's head.

61. *Lady in red.* There's nothing like a slinky red dress, spandex if possible, to bring out the vamp in you. Imagine you're doing an erotic hootchy-kootchy atop some foreign bar, the music hot and driving, while the entire club cheers and collectively breathes heavily. Locking eyes with your rapt audience, you pull your tight dress up to a slightly indecent level so your legs can crouch, high-kick, and spread for balance. My friend Claudia, who actually did this in Thailand, said her husband will never forget it. 'I thought I might have to die that night, defending her honor,' he told me. 'But if so, I would die happy.'

62. *Lap dance.* Just like in the girlie bars, the man sits in a chair while you, clad only in skimpy lingerie, prance all around him, oozing seduction. Here's your chance to walk the fine line between goddess and trollop. He is forbidden to touch you, but you can tease him at will. Sit right on top of his clothed lap and roll your hips – either frontward, with pelvic mound, or backward, with plump bottom. Slap his hand if he attempts to relieve his ache by caressing you.

Striptease 101

The best description I've ever seen of a teasing strip comes from Anaïs Nin's *Delta of Venus:*

First she loosened her wild hair, shook it like a mane . . . Her hands were slow and caressing. She did not handle herself objectively, but like a woman ascertaining with her hands the exact condition of her body, patting it in gratitude for its perfections. One gesture opened the shoulders and let [her] dress fall over her breasts but no further. At this point she decided to look at her face mirror and examine her eyelashes. Then she opened the zipper which exposed the ribs, the beginning of the breasts, the beginning of the belly's curve . . . [She] had a way of shaking herself, as if to loosen her muscles . . . This shake, which ran through her body, gave the breasts an air of being handled with violence. Then she took the dress lightly at the hem and lifted it slowly over her shoulders . . . stuck for a moment. Something caught with her long hair . . . The body which emerged . . . startled them by the sensuality in every curve . . . She wore black stockings, and high leather boots. As she struggled with the boots, she was at the mercy of anyone who approached her . . . She continued to struggle with the entangled dress, shaking herself as if in a spasm of love. Finally, she freed herself, after the students had satisfied their eyes.

- Remember, it's the *tease* that's important.
- Key movements are: arching your back, pointing your toes, gliding your hands over your body, slithering as you smooth clothes off.

- Pause occasionally to lock eyes; then roll your tongue around your lips and throw a kiss.
- Excite yourself as well as your audience by cupping your naked breasts, bottom, and pelvic triangle as you disrobe. Pinch and squeeze them, showing them off.
- Throw your leg over the top of a chair to land a high-heeled foot on the chair seat.
- Offer him your discarded panties and bra. Wrap your stockings around his erection. Caress it with your empty shoe.
- Reveal your body as if it's a fine work of art.

playthings

Toys designed for sensual pleasure have been around for centuries – from carved dildos found in Egyptian tombs to eighteenth-century French ticklers to today's high-powered vibrators molded in the likeness of porn stars. Passion Triggers extraordinaire, they can be a marvelous way to expand the opportunities for variety, play, and adventure in any intimate relationship – whether you shop for them together, imagining all the wild possibilities that await, or surprise him by hiding a new sexual bauble at the bottom of your picnic basket.

63. *Toys for his tool.* Combining modern technology with ancient pleasure secrets, latex or rubber rings and sleeves are designed to enhance sensation for both of you. By wrapping a stretchy ring around the base of your man's love spear, you provide him with a delicious feel of restriction and a larger, longer-lasting erection. Many pleasure rings sport knobs that stimulate his penile pressure points and your external love organs. The sleeves that completely encase his member usually have larger beads all over, or even plumes on the end, to ripple delightfully inside you and give him the feel of a thousand little tongues lapping on his shaft. Buy a few erection-huggers and experiment to see what really tickles both of you.

64. Introduce your man to the thrill of intense pulsation by giving him a sensual massage with your vibrator. Circle over his shoulders, back, and arms, slowly moving on to tingle his thighs and behind. Alternate feathery and long firm strokes with your teasing circles, and mix in some kisses and soft nibbles, too. When he's ready, try a light throb on his nipples and then the sensitive areas near his genitals, always keeping skin contact with your hand, mouth, breasts, or pubis. Before he wants you to, put the vibrator aside and leave him lusting for more.

65. When he is making love to you from behind, press a vibrator to your thighs, pelvic mound, or clitoris. Besides inflaming you, it also

transmits tinging pulsations to his erection right through the walls of your throbbing flesh.

66. Lay a vibrator against your cheek while you are giving him oral sex.

67. Cradle his testicles in one hand and roll your vibrator gently but insistently across his perineum. Keep his penis hot and happy with your mouth or hand as you pulsate from perineum to scrotum and around the base of his flaming sword.

68. Wrap your panties around the vibrator or his shivering shaft to soften the intensity when you apply your pulsing love toy directly to his member.

69. Hold only his glans in your mouth and sweep a vibrator slowly up and down on the hypersensitive underside ridge of his love weapon.

70. In the missionary, or woman-on-top, position, snuggle a vibrator between your pelvises and let him thrill to the electric oscillations against his pubis as well as your intensified orgasmic shudders around his penetrating root.

4

the holy harlot

Here in this body are the sacred rivers; here are the sun and moon, as well as all the pilgrimage places. I have not encountered another temple as blissful as my own body.

—*Saraha Doha*

In ancient times, when god was a woman, men stood in awe of the ineffable mysteries of the female body – childbirth, the production of life-giving milk, her bleeding in rhythm with the moon, the magical power to make a man's organ rise, and her seemingly infinite capacity for sexual pleasure. While every woman was respected and cherished, those who were dedicated to the service of the Great Mother were considered actual embodiments of the Goddess, able to invoke Her love, ecstasy, and fertility through acts of sacred sexual union.

These long-ago love priestesses were women who knew the sacred power of their bodies and used it boldly. In ancient Greece, well-educated and refined courtesans were among the most respected women of that culture. In India, the temple prostitutes were worshiped, their very name meaning 'handmaid of god.' And the 'Joy Maidens' of Ishtar (Babylon) and Inanna (Sumeria) bestowed the sexual favors of the Goddess in order to elevate men to a divine state and to anoint earthly kings with the legitimate power to rule. In these and many other ways, everyone honored the Great Mother, who had gifted her children with the joy of sacred sexuality.

We can reclaim the mystery and sacredness of our erotic natures by taking a cue from these ancient women. If we view our bodies with devotion and assert our natural right to divine pleasure, we will begin to embody our venerable heritage. At least in the bedroom, we will once again wield our power to transform, initiate, and enlighten.

reclaiming our bodies

A powerful aura surrounds the woman who loves her own body, and she becomes a deliciously dangerous weapon of love. She uses her curvy breasts and hips, her natural musky scents, her vast orgasmic capacity, and her inborn sensuality to trigger her own passion as well as seduce and delight her lucky man.

71. *Self-pleasuring – the key to being a great lover.* A sex goddess is a woman who is intimate with the secrets of her own body – and, as she chooses, reveals those mysteries to her lover. Take the time to learn firsthand how sensitive your nipples are, where your clitoris meets your labial lips and how it likes to be massaged, whether you respond better to hard, fast thrusts or slow, gentle strokes. Pleasure yourself to the point of no return every day for a week before finally releasing into an explosive climax – a week during which you will be glowing and seductively magnetic. Start a burning fire in your lover's loins by letting him watch and learn. When you find out for yourself what your throbbing contractions feel like to a man, and how sexy you look with nipples erect and hips undulating, you will have a visceral feel for the high-wattage power that is yours to

command – and the pride and daring of a holy harlot to use it.

72. *24-hour-a-day sensuality.* Our physical senses are the doorways through which we take in beauty and pour out romance. If we consciously tune into them, their messages trigger our inner passions and translate into more sensual acts of loving. Luxuriate in the smell of a gardenia. Eat a succulent fig. Wear silk. Notice the color changes in your man's body when he becomes aroused. Taste his love sweat. Become enraptured with the heady aroma of your lovemaking. Accessorize your sexplay with fur massage mitts, juicy fruits, stunning bed costumes, and musky love oils. When you allow your senses to open, the barriers to full-bodied eroticism fall away and you become a creature of devastating sensual impulse – exciting, inventive, and primally seductive.

73. *Bosom of the goddess.* *Playboy* magazine has made fortunes capitalizing on men's obsession with breasts. We can repossess that dowry by holding the power of our satin orbs in our own hands. First, let him look but not touch as you lift and squeeze each one to show off its plump succulence. Still cupping one globe, slowly pluck at, twist, and engorge the dark and alluring nipple. Your own passion now rising, undulate toward him while pressing your pearly spheres together

with circular massage strokes. Then cradle and raise each prize to his lips, finally allowing him to suckle and delight the ripe, round jewels he is now mad to possess.

Claiming Your Orgasm

The Original Idea

Comes from the Greek word *orgas*, meaning 'to swell,' and the Sanskrit *urg*, meaning 'nourishment, power, strength.' Imagine the event as a rich swelling of your body, emotions, and female power.

Why It Matters

You could fake it, but why miss out? Asserting that you want and deserve full pleasure makes a strikingly sexy statement. Furthermore, orgasm enhances your feeling of aliveness and produces a hormone called oxytocin, which increases lust. And for your man, nothing is more erotic and empowering than knowing he has driven his woman over the edge into ecstasy.

Triggering a Climax

Though it is sometimes elusive, you can deliberately coax your body into orgasm by doing things that bring blood and sensitivity to the area:

1. Pant, imagining that you are breathing into your vagina.
2. Tighten your buttocks, especially the anal muscles.
3. Massage your clitoris directly, either with your own or your lover's hand.
4. Invite him to lick you.
5. Clench and release your PC muscles.
6. Push out forcefully and hold.
7. Stress your thigh muscles by leaning back from a standing or kneeling posture.
8. Get into positions that encourage deep penetration and intense G-spot or clitoral stimulation – you on top; deep, free-moving rear entry; missionary with a pillow under your bottom.

The Sound of One Orgasm Happening

Your man might never know how wild and blissful he's made you unless you tell him. Moan, growl, scream in ecstasy. Kiss and thank him for the most incredible orgasm you've ever had. Don't be afraid to go overboard with cries of pleasure and words of praise; they help you express and intensify your rapture while making him feel manly, potent, and inspired.

74. ***The scent of a woman.*** A woman's natural perfume is a vital part of her magical power. The smell of your clean hair, skin, love secretions, and the clothes you've recently worn can all be potent aphrodisiacs that unlock the doors to your own, as well as your man's, primal passion. Leave the negligee you made love in last night on his pillow or drop it in his briefcase. Snuggle your clean hair against his mouth and nose. Daub your own love juices like cologne between your warm breasts.

75. ***Theater of the mind.*** When your mind is aflame with erotic imaginings, your body emits rays of hot passion. To take your desire and magnetism to new levels, make your fantasies overly lush and romantic or bold and raunchy in the extreme. Tantric lovers of yore imagined that beaming lovelight poured from their nipples and that similar to a man's Arrow of Love, their clitorises pulsated with erect female potency. In ancient Rome, women paid exorbitant prices for the sweat that was scraped off the bodies of gladiators and made into dream-inducing inhalants and facial packs. The women of classical Greece would fancy themselves as Aphrodite or Helen of Troy, full of secret knowledge and irresistible magic, hot ambrosia flooding their breasts and wombs. To be queen of your erotic imagination is to exert a powerful rule over the responses of both your body and your man's.

reclaiming the sacred vulva

From Paleolithic cave art to eleventh-century Indian and Balinese sculptures, from Sheela-Na-Gigs carved on medieval European churches to figures of female genitalia found in Greek, Siberian, and Bolivian temples, the vulva has for many ages been a universal religious icon representing the holiest of all mysteries. Revering it as the magical portal of life and the place where the phallus finds bliss and illumination, worshipers would touch the sacred stone triangle or painted womb to receive the blessing and potent fecundity it radiated.

Today, though some of its symbolic luster has dimmed, the magic and awesome power of a woman's vulva still remains. It will always be the most intimate chamber, in which we cradle our unborn children as well as the male essence of our lovers. It is the source of our mystery and the repository of all our feelings about being female. For men, it is the Holy Grail they endlessly lust after but can never really possess. If we women were to venerate our own wombs and ardently believe in their magic once again, it would transform the nature of who we are and how we relate to our lovers.

76. *Vagina awareness.* You will be surprised at the difference in your sensations and his attention level when you practice being awed by your female equipment. Several times a day, think about how warm and voluptuous your womb is, how 'all magic radiates from it as fingers do from a hand.' Do a few hula or belly-dance movements in the mirror, just to admire, loosen, and sense the femaleness of your hot inner flower. Go without panties for a solid week and feel your vulval skin being awakened and tantalized by air, fabric, and friction. When you are near your man, remember that, as the sex therapist Jude Cotter, Ph.D., says, 'in all mammals, the male is very attendant to the vagina. He wants to see it, touch it, smell it, taste it.' Let your pelvis radiate the psychic steam of that knowledge.

77. *Displaying your hibiscus.* Perhaps because our wombs hold a secret no one fully understands, men find the sight of a woman holding her sex lips wide open intensely erotic and beautiful. If you boldly spread your genital flower wide as he approaches to kiss or penetrate you there, you will increase the sensitivity of your labia and clitoris while driving him insane with lust.

78. *PC milking.* One of the most ancient of the arts practiced by the original holy harlots was that of milking the man's Rainbow Serpent with their talented vaginal muscles. If you practice contracting your PCs twenty-five to fifty times

every day, you will soon have the gripping power of a boa constrictor and the lusty appetite of a tigress in heat (the internal clenching stimulates your clitoris, engorges your love tunnel, and sends pleasurable nerve messages to your brain). With practice, you can accomplish the famed and highly coveted milking trick by separately squeezing the outer-muscle group at the vaginal opening, the middle muscles further up the canal, and finally the inner band near the anus in a perpetually rolling motion.

79. *PC pump.* Grip him with your inner muscles and hold for about three heartbeats. Then quickly clench a little tighter and release. Pause for three more heartbeats and repeat. After several rounds, accelerate your pace by holding for only two heartbeats, then one, then constantly pumping till he screams for mercy.

80. *The Goddess-spot.* The ancient love sages of Rome, India, Egypt, and the Orient considered the G-spot to be the sacred wellspring of a woman's magical power. It is located along the sensitive upper lining of the vaginal canal – very often about two inches inside and just above the curve of the pubic bone. Explore with your own finger (it's swollen and easier to find when you're aroused) until you touch something that feels like it's at the very center of your womanly being. Once you locate it, invite your man to unlock its oceanic orgasms and mysterious initiatory power

through deep, insistent massage or well-placed thrusts. (Doggie-style and woman-on-top positions are best.) Though the G-spot requires prolonged stimulation, many women find that once it's awakened, their hips undulate almost involuntarily, they become multiorgasmic, and their deepest primal impulses are unleashed. But it's not just your wild shudders that will mesmerize him. As the original love priestesses knew, a G-spot orgasm releases some ineffable essence that makes you both feel as though the earth has not only moved, but actually cracked open to reveal a new paradise.

81. *Vulva-speak.* Like Baubo, a goddess who saw through her nipples and talked from between her legs, you can actually transmit and receive messages with your agile and effusive vagina. Putting all your attention in your womb, imagine that it has the eyes and ears of love. Then mentally ask his swollen virility to reveal its personality and wants to you. If it says, 'I am handsome and brave, and love to go hunting in the far corners of your luscious vagina,' you'll be able to give him the perfect hero's welcome. If it divulges, 'I love it when you caress me with your nails and teeth,' you'll know exactly how to fulfill his unspoken desires. Speak to his man-thing with your vulva, sending all your love and passion out through its pores directly onto his sensitive penile skin. Your erotic messages will bathe his manhood with liquid tingles he just can't get enough of.

reclaiming our position of power

One of the most characteristic poses of the ancient Great Goddess is the open-thighed squat. Statues of Isis show her squatting with gown hitched up, proudly revealing her role as the dispenser of the fruits of life. She also crouches over her husband, Osiris, to reattach his dismembered phallus. The Indian goddess Kali perches atop Shiva in order to give him the gift of enlightenment. And Inanna, the Sumerian Goddess of Heaven and Earth and the original Holy Harlot, is seen in many plaques squatting in the act of ritual sexual union that renews the fertility of Her lands.

This posture, which I call the Sumerian Squat, puts things in their proper perspective. You are in control of your own pleasure and all the action. Your man can switch from concentrating on physical movement to focusing on emotional ecstasy, as you take on your true role of sexual initiatrix. Much different from the kneeling woman-on-top position, here your whole body is freely mobile and your 'wondrous vulva' is magnificently displayed. And because your inner lips are spread open and your thigh muscles stressed, you increase the sensitivity and sexual charge in your genital area.

82. *The Full Sumerian Squat.* Stand regally over your prone man so he can worship the

proud beauty of your entire body. Tease him with the prize that is to come by undulating your hips, displaying and caressing your sacred vulva, talking about how hot it is for him and what it is about to do. Slowly lower your body into a squatting position atop his waiting sword and impale yourself upon it. Bounce your torso up and down, back and forth, or around in circles with the springiness of your legs. Freely stroke your body and breasts as well as his chest, testicles, and thighs. Take your pleasure fully, knowing that you are giving him the most erotic show on earth and driving his swollen spear mad with desire.

83. *The Reverse Sumerian Squat.* Stand astride with your back to him, giving him a ripe view of your bottom. Stroke it lovingly with your hands and perhaps bend over slightly so he can glimpse the treasure between your legs. Sink slowly over his upright sex and squeeze him with your PCs a few times. Use both your hands and feet to push off as you raise and lower yourself provocatively. This position affords extreme penetration and marvelous stimulation of your Goddess-spot.

84. *The Sumerian Tease.* As you hover above his weapon, make a long, drawn-out tease of inserting it. Scrape your fingernails over his chest, belly, and penis, perhaps giving it a light, promising kiss. Clasp his magic wand and slide the head across the entire length of your open vaginal

lips, making a little circle around your clitoris. Insert only the glans and clench your PCs around it. Then raise yourself to let the head slip out and revert to caressing the rest of his body or yours. Next time, let his sword in a little further, squeeze a few times, and edge it out once again. Repeat your slow torture, going a little deeper each time until you finally lower yourself over the full length of his now-quivering lance.

85. *The Sumerian Knee Lock.* Raise his knees to his chest, then crouch and mount him by bringing your knees outside of his and sitting on his derriere. His calves surround your torso, and your hands rest on his chest for support as you bob up and down, keeping his knees locked between your elbows and lower thighs. Makes for a very interesting angle of penetration.

86. *The Spiral of Nines.* This is a thrusting sequence that men have used to thrill their women for centuries. But now that you're on top, you can do the exotic driving. As you spring up and down, develop a rhythm of varied thrusts – three shallow and one quick, deep engulfment; then five shallow and one deep; seven shallow, one deep; and finally nine shallow and one eagerly anticipated full-bore thrust. Keep up the nine-to-one pattern, gasping with joy each time you plunge him deeply within, until one of you reaches nirvana.

87. *Inanna's Throne.* With him sitting in a chair, stand on the chair seat, feet astride his thighs. Descend slowly, perhaps offering your succulent oyster to his lips before embracing his thick shank in your glistening depths. Swivel a few times, kissing and nibbling at his mouth. Then grasp the arms of the chair for leverage, and push yourself up and down upon his deeply implanted scepter.

88. *Inanna's Throne Reversed.* He sits in an armless chair, and you, standing on the floor facing away from him, lower yourself over his lap. Wind your legs around the outside of his. From here you can: (1) bounce up and down, using your feet on the floor and hands on his knees for leverage, while he assists by cupping your behind; (2) arch gracefully back and wrap your hands around his neck, while he has free rein to reach around and caress your jutting nipples and spread-eagled sex flower; (3) grind atop him as you tickle his testicles (and your own love bud) with your fingertips; or (4) lean forward to grasp his ankles and rock back and forth. Exquisite depth of penetration and G-spot stimulation.

89. *Isis Revealed.* Have him sit on a fairly plump pillow on the floor, his feet up close to his bottom and his hands on the floor to brace himself. Facing him, straddle his hips, your feet planted on the floor beside them. Lean back and put your arms straight out behind you so your hands

support you on the floor. You can now rock your whole body forward and back, or thrust your hips into the air and fall down upon his shaft at will. You enjoy superb G-spot stimulation while he delights in a magnificent view of your spread-open love nest and boldly distended bosom.

90. *Two Tails Kissing.* He lies on his back with knees to his chest. With your back to him, impale yourself on his stiffened spear by sitting on his rump and the backs of his thighs. For bouncing support, rest your hands on the bed or lean back to clasp his arms. He can add leverage by positioning his feet on the backs of your shoulders. The rubbing together of your two bottoms and the exotic angle of penetration will provide both of you with previously unknown delights.

5

how did you get into that position?

Intercourse is not primarily an experience of personal love, but of the gods, which yet happens through the union of two. The partner is no longer felt to be limited to the familiar conscious personality, but has become also the gateway to the infinite mystery of life.

—*Eleanor Bertine*

Even if only subconsciously, men cherish the idea that women's bodies hold some kind of secret that, when finally penetrated, will reveal the meaning of their lives. And, of course, they're right. By inviting him into your body, you are literally opening the gates of heaven. Entranced and elevated by the act of love, you become the Keeper of the Keys – guardian and guide to a realm of rapturous mystery he cannot possibly enter on his own. It is a land where penetration becomes revelation, thrusting becomes ritualistic fire-making, and sexual positions are transformed into the postures that conjure ecstasy.

Fortunately, you don't need to become a pretzel to achieve these positions of goddesslike power. The mere act of opening your legs, if done with a sense of purpose, can raise both yours and your man's temperatures considerably. So don't simply allow him to penetrate you; entwine him in your aphrodisiacal embrace, engulf his manhood with your hot oceanic vagina, offer him the secrets of your scent. Like the moon, your mysterious body has the power to drive a man crazy simply by moving through his sky. Use it to design irresistible sculptures of desire.

opening the doors of paradise

91. Make his initial entry into your body feel like admission to the alcove of a temple. If you breathe out fully in preparation, then inhale and contract your PC muscles as his manly member crosses your threshold, he will feel inexorably sucked into your velvety abyss. Conversely, by tightening your PCs beforehand and then releasing them as he enters, you will create the sensation that your hothouse flower is blooming voluptuously for him.

92. Take hold of his weapon to guide it partway into your sanctuary. Then move your hands to his pelvis, stopping his progress. Let him begin thrusting, then suddenly release your obstructing hands so that he falls unexpectedly into your moist, deep cave.

93. Imagine that your vagina is a hot mouth, actually kissing your lover's phallic essence. Your hips will naturally move more sinuously, your inner muscles will caress and suck on his love spear, and he will feel as though you are awakening his true manhood.

94. While he is thrusting, place your fingers at the base of his kingly shaft. Holding down the

loose skin will keep it taut and almost unbearably sensitized.

missionary magic

95. *Saucy Missionary.* Spread your legs wide in brazen invitation. As he ogles you and assumes the familiar missionary position, open your legs even wider and tilt your hips up. The extension and angle expose more of your clitoris and inner lips to his thrusting pelvic bone.

96. *Cross His Heart.* In the basic missionary position, raise your knees to your shoulders, cross your ankles, and place your feet on his chest. This affords you great G-spot stimulation, while your feet energize the love hormones around his heart. Further, if you can lower your crossed ankles to the tummy area and pull his weight down onto them, the increased pressure to both your and your man's genitals will send spirits soaring.

97. *Missionary Zeal.* With your legs braced around his *upper* back, slide your arms around his neck and coo into his ear, 'Darling, stay still just a moment.' Then, using your limbs as leverage, sway your pelvis freely upon his fulcrum in undulating circles and rhythmic teeter-totters.

98. *Missionary Squeeze.* When you're in the missionary position with your knees draped over his shoulders, straighten your legs and bring them toward your breast. By crossing your calves, you compress your vaginal lips tightly around his holy scepter.

99. *Elvis Missionary I.* Situate yourself on the bed so you can prop your feet against the wall or headboard, knees bent. He kneels into the missionary posture. With your weight supported by your shoulders on the bed and your feet on the wall, your airborne hips can swivel, swing, and bounce as wildly as the 'King' ever dared. Because this freewheeling movement replicates the pattern of energy that flows through your body during orgasm, you are actually encouraging the buildup of your own passionate tension.

100. *Elvis Missionary II.* Let your behind dangle off the edge of the bed, while your supplicant kneels on the floor between your open legs. Bolstering yourself with feet firmly planted on the floor, you can again gyrate your pelvis with orgiastic abandon. Hallelujah!

101. *Elvis Missionary III.* Plop yourself seductively on a desk or table near a wall, rump cascading over the edge, feet planted wide apart on the wall. Invite your lover to stand in the crotch of your V-ed legs and enter the portals of heaven. *Both* of you can rock and bump freely, all

hands are free for pinching and caressing, and your G-spot is in line for delicious direct contact.

102. *Pile-Drivin' Missionary.* My fiery, red-haired friend Camille reported this as one of the wildest rides of her life. After testing it out myself, I had to agree. Starting from the missionary position, drape your legs over his shoulders. He raises himself upright on his knees, keeping himself inserted by elevating your hips. With your feet now braced on his shoulders, legs straight, he grasps your ankles and, by driving them like a human hammer, pumps you up and down on his throbbing piston.

side ways

103. *Coy Hussy.* You lie on your side in the fetal position. He kneels beside your derriere and inserts his impudent weapon, which will strike you in invigorating new spots. While you give him coy sideways glances, offering yourself without spreading your legs, he revels in the tighter fit and spectacular view.

104. *Thigh-Buster.* Lie on your side and slip your bottom leg between his thighs, your other leg atop his shoulder. While he can masterfully glide you up and down on him by grasping

your top leg and luscious rump, you can assist by raising and lowering your bottom thigh. Great for firming that nasty flab.

105. *Deep Wrap.* If you entwine both legs around his waist while you are lying side by side, face-to-face, you will greatly increase the depth of his penetration and the level of your ecstasy.

106. *Long, Slow Scissors.* Imagine two pairs of open scissors locking together. If each of you props yourself up from a prone position with your right and his left elbows, you can easily reach your lover's inner thighs and genitals as well as gaze smolderingly into each other's eyes. Movement consists of the easy sliding and rocking of hips and the clenching of your spirited PC muscles. This posture is so relaxed that you can go on for delirious, long hours, even feeding each other a sexy meal or reading love poetry while remaining hotly entangled.

standing ovation

107. *Stand by Your Woman.* Sit on the edge of a bed or soft chair and invite your man to stand between your legs. Clasp your thighs around his waist, or even his chest, and lie back to rest your weight on your shoulders. Instructing him to cradle your cheeks with his hands, arch your back and bounce your pelvis up and down

on his erect appendage. He will adore being your support and eyeballing all your sexy gyrations.

108. *Tarzan and Jane.* Find something high and sturdy to hang on to – door frame, tree limb, shower bar or nozzle, coatrack, etc. The two of you approach from opposite sides, grasp the bar with both hands, and lean back with hips taut and touching. Arms stretched high overhead, pelvises locked together, and with the suspended freedom of wild creatures swinging through the trees, you can make juicy jungle love.

109. *Zambian Shoulder Stand.* The sexually astute Zambian elders of Africa promote this as the position offering deeper penetration than any other. Starting from a shoulder stand, you lower your feet to the bed or floor behind your head. You are supporting your weight on your shoulders, elbows, and toes, your glistening pomegranate shamelessly exposed. He approaches on his knees, between your feet, and plunges himself deeply into your ultimate fruit. In this posture, the erotic undulation of your hips will squeeze your PC muscles for you, and the stretching of your long thigh and rump muscles enhances the fierceness of your orgasmic contractions.

from the rear

110. *Rearview Mirror.* Miss the face-to-face intimacy when you're doing it doggie style? Positioning yourself next to a large mirror enables you to ogle the action for a change, him to view your ecstatic expressions, and both of you to have meaningful reflected eye contact.

111. *Sit and Conquer.* Start out in the doggie position and then lustily push his hips back and down with your rear, so he is sitting on his heels (supporting himself with his hands on the bed behind him). You will be sort of squatting over him and can either rock to and fro, still leaning forward with hands on the bed, or sit up and bounce. The extra tension in his thighs will triple the sensation and energy flowing to his captive genitals.

112. *Come and Get It.* Mount a soft chair from the front, one knee on each chair arm and forearms resting on the chair back. Your spread-eagled legs, creamy globes at just the right height for his standing thrusts, and freely undulating hips, offer him a penetrating invitation he can't refuse.

113. *Same Dog, New Tricks.* To add a little zest to the plain old rear-entry position, slide your fingers down to the soft spot just above your

pubic mound and press in. As you massage, he will feel increased pressure. Then place the V of two fingers over your pulsing bud, the fingers themselves resting on the lips of your honeyed flower. Squeeze, knead, and caress yourself around his hard stem in rhythm with your surging pelvis.

114. *Slave of Love.* Transform yourself into a servant girl being taken by her master and reap the lordly results. In the doggie pose, fold your hands in the nape of your neck and press your face and chest to the bed. Then draw him very deep inside you by wrapping your legs tightly around his thighs and squeezing. You may want to plead ecstatically, as Annette Bening did in *American Beauty,* 'Fuck me, Your Majesty!'

encores

115. The best way to re-harden a man for more pleasure is, no surprise, fervent oral sex. Sponging him off with a warm flannel in between adds a nice touch to this. But many men respond better to having their nipples licked or their entire body caressed – it's as though, after all that other activity, the rest of his body is finally super-sensitive. And sometimes it's the vision of you pleasuring yourself that makes him rock-hard once again. After giving him a few minutes to gather strength, coo words of adoration and press your body against his. Try a stroke here and a kiss

there, staying alert for latent sparks of electricity. If the flesh is willing, it will happily spring to attention once more, considering itself blessed to have such a lusty, insatiable woman.

116. A re-stiffening trick used by professional women, this works best when you're on top. After he's cooled down from his climax, raise yourself so only the tip of his sated member remains inside you and hold it there with your PCs. Caressing his thighs and belly with one hand, use the other to slide the loose penile skin up, down, and around his shaft, gently kneading and teasing until signs of new life appear.

Better Sex Through Technology

- **Rhythm control**. To get his fast and your slower orgasmic paces more in line, use some breathing techniques. By panting fast, you will quicken and enhance your arousal. Conversely, if he inhales deeply and slowly, his rapid pulsing will decelerate – perhaps allowing you to peak simultaneously for a change.
- **Squeeze and please**. To temporarily delay his inevitable eruption (and prolong his and your pleasure), try any of these: (1) Delicately encircle the area just above his testicles and pull down gently, holding for ten to thirty seconds; (2) press two fingers

firmly into his perineum for about ten breaths; (3) squeeze firmly just below the head or at the very base of his shaft. The latter is the most surefire technique, but the advantage of the first two is that they can be performed while he remains inside you. And, as always, different strokes work for different folks.

- **Raincoat application.** If you put it on, the process becomes a pleasure instead of a chore. First, put a dollop of water-based lubricant in the tip and stretch the rim a little. Then position it at the tip of his weapon with one hand while you caress him to erection with the other. As he grows into it, circle your fingers above the rim of the condom and roll it all the way down, making sure to leave enough room at the tip to catch his spurting love fluids.

6

phallus worship

As an apple tree in the forest

Is my beloved among men.

I sit beneath his shadow

And taste his sweet, ripe fruit.

I am weak with passion.

—*Song of Songs*

part i: the oral tradition

There's the thing that men get into pissing contests with, obsess over the size of, and that often deprives them of the capacity for reason. Then there's the Shaft of Eros. The shivering truncheon of his sex. The thunderbolt of Shiva. A torch so hot it can only be quenched by your lips and vulva. Which one would you rather cuddle up to at night? Which would you prefer to be ravished by?

As the magician of love that you are, you have the power to transform your man's proudest possession into any one of these. Something that will mesmerize you with desire and trigger your deepest passions. Something that will inspire him to penetrate you with sweet, unbearable agony until your toes shudder. You choose.

The simple key to giving great oral sex, and getting insanely turned on by it, is to worship his Golden Scepter of Love. Passion Trigger supreme, it is the earthy, holy thing that exudes virility, power, courage, creativity, and life's mysterious potency. Let it intrigue and astound you. Adore it, caress it, name it, adorn it, swoon over it as if it were a piece of Belgian chocolate. If you see, smell, and taste it that way, you will both be in a delirium of ecstasy. Out of your lust, you will invent sinfully delicious new licks and sucks. And he will be helplessly smitten.

Penis Secret #1: A man's penis is the key to his heart. Unlike a woman's sexuality, which encompasses her entire body and is at least as emotional as it is physical, a man's sexuality is centered in this one physical organ. Licking him there will touch him emotionally and deeply bond the two of you.

Penis Secret #2: If you *begin* by paying your loving respects to the Lizard King first, sometimes kissing it even before you kiss his mouth, you can then travel freely to other parts of his body. Gradually, this will initiate him into full-body eroticism.

Penis Secret #3: According to the Mayflower Madam, the call girl's secret to a great blow job is enthusiasm. Men say, 'It was great. She *loves* it!'

Penis Secret #4: Having trouble developing Penis Lust? Try *receiving* it with your mouth instead of *giving* oral sex. *You* feel the sensations without worrying about his. Let your tongue and inner lips feel the silkiness of your man's rod of love, its swollen ripeness, its hot-iron quality. Taste its unique personality, and it will come alive for you.

117. Words are powerful aphrodisiacs. Let your man's love instrument be a frequent topic of conversation. Several times a day tell him how gorgeous it is, how much it thrills you, how hard and mighty it is, how much you love to suck it. Without having to do anything physical, you've warmed his blood as well as yours.

118. When you first approach your lover's organ, it may still be soft and tender. Start by licking only the head, very gently as a cat's tongue would. As he begins to stiffen, delicately suck it into your mouth with just your lips. Then swallow, creating a tantalizing wave of pressure on the tip. When he's fully erect, you can suck on the whole shaft as if it were hard candy.

119. Start licking his eager rabbit even *before* he gets his pants off. Lean down and breathe warm air against him, right through his briefs. Then wet the cloth with your tongue and slither it up and down his pulsing shaft. I've heard one man claim this was the most erotic thing that ever happened to him.

120. *Snake Charmer's Position.* Placement can be crucial. Since men love to watch, make sure to place yourself so he can *see* his Big Serpent dancing in and out of your mouth. The star of the classic porn film *Behind the Green*

Door added a beautiful flourish to this. Naked and kneeling, she would allow her whole body to undulate, each suck cascading sensuously from mouth to breasts to pelvis to toes. Truly a mesmerizing vision.

121. *Queen's Position.* Relax on a throne of pillows so that your head is raised. Beckon him to kneel astride your breasts while you pleasure him orally. Or lie flat and command him to lower himself over your royal lips, leaning forward onto his elbows for support.

122. *Tantric Nun Position.* According to Tantric texts, the rapture of orgasm is greatly enhanced when one's head is hanging down. Position your man so that his head and upper torso dangle off the edge of the bed. Kneel at his head, offering your vagina to his lips if he cares to partake, lean forward, and devour his Sacred Scepter.

123. *Dominatrix Position.* Spread his limbs out on the bed. Pin down his wrists with your two feet, and, parking your hands firmly on his thighs (for support and to keep them spread), let your tongue show him who's mistress.

124. The danger of discovery is a lovely spice for any sensual meal. Cars, elevators, parks, alleyways, secluded beaches, his locked office, or

even someone else's bathroom are all perfect for surprise lip attacks. One friend managed to maroon her boyfriend in an opera house lobby, just after everyone had gone back in for Act II. She said the taste of his tension, as he tried to remain silent and sedate, was thrillingly delicious.

125. The chilled heat of minty toothpaste, mentholated cough drops, Binaca, or Altoids on your tongue feels divine to any penis. Sexy Frenchwomen are famous for their crème de menthe 'cocktails.' Try putting some of the cooling liqueur in your mouth and letting it spill over the head of his member before your lips slowly descend. Once he's all the way inside your mouth, exhale warm air onto his cooled skin. Expect shudders.

126. *Pinch of Pleasure.* Here's how the ladies in the harems of Rajasthan increase their raja's pleasure. A soft pinch to the loose skin at the base of the penis causes the rest of the covering skin to be pulled taut (especially important if he's uncircumcised). Holding it there while you lick sensually all over the now-sensitized head will kindle fire in the desert.

127. My vixenish, flame-haired friend Karen revealed her much ballyhooed technique. She keeps her tongue very wide and firm, places it at his perineum, and in one slow lick, travels across the scrotal sac and all the way up his fleshy

spear. At the spear point, she circles, flicks, and laps with her tongue, maybe slipping him briefly into her mouth. Repeat this as many times as needed.

128. *Mars Butterfly.* You've heard of the Venus Butterfly? Well, here's the male version. Flutter your hard tongue back and forth across that inviting slit in his glans. Mercilessly. If you hold the slit open just a bit with your fingers, you'll really send him flying.

129. When you have his lovely lance in your mouth, your tongue should be moving constantly. That's what creates the *real* stimulation. Swirl it around the entire shaft or just the tip. Lick back and forth just under the rim. A fellatio specialist at one Japanese sex club said her secret is to lap at the base until his penis shudders.

130. Occasionally tease him by removing your mouth. Then stick the hard tip of your tongue into the slit and vibrate.

131. Use the hard palate on the roof of your mouth to provide additional stimulation. By tipping the glans up and forward, you can slide it tantalizingly across those ripply ridges.

132. For a little variety, grasp the head of his throbbing, slippery appendage in one hand and then nip delicately all along the shank. Let your fangs be gentle.

133. Apply a Tantric thrusting technique to your tongue work. After sucking only the tip for a while, suddenly give his organ one full stroke to the bottom with your hungry mouth. Follow by teasing just the head again. Then three full strokes. Lick the head. Five full strokes, head only, and so on. Keep increasing the temperature by two strokes until 'done.'

134. You know how just a tiny bit of fluid seeps from the tip when he's really excited? I love to collect this delicious nectar with my tongue and deposit it in my lover's mouth with a kiss. I close my eyes and murmur, 'Mmmm, taste this.' Keep your hand sliding over his limb while your mouth is otherwise occupied. This encourages full participation. Repeat as desired.

135. *Fire and Ice.* Hot rod and cold tongue make a scintillating combo. Melt a piece of ice in your mouth, then swallow him up. Or use the frosty cube to caress his testicles while your warm lips encase his shivering shaft. If you want to cause real havoc, wait to ice his balls until just before he's ready to spout. Be ready for an exciting eruption!

136. ***Fire and Ice II.*** While performing fellatio, occasionally pause to sip some hot tea or coffee, cold juice, or icy beer. Swirl the liquid around to inundate every corner of your mouth before lowering your lips over him again. Alternate temperatures; men love contrast.

137. ***Fire and Ice III.*** When his lance is afire, smooth on some chocolate ice cream. Obviously, you then devour and conquer.

138. While you are sucking him, put your finger in your mouth and tickle his penis with it. Then slide your wet finger down to massage his perineum or backside bud.

139. Once you have him deep in your throat, pull back slowly, sucking hard. Leave just the tip in your mouth as you massage his shaft with one hand and tweedle his perineum or anus with the other.

140. Give his greedy member full coverage. Because your mouth can't encase all of him the whole time, augment with your hands. Either suck and pull in opposite directions, or attach your encircling fingers to your lips and move them up and down in tandem. He won't be able to distinguish between mouth and hands, and will believe you to be Wonder Woman.

141. *Tinfoil Hum Job.* My girlfriend Chris, an innocent-looking little pixie, highly recommends this wild technique. Wrap aluminum foil around his testicles, put your lips over them, and hum. The foil adds heat, intensity, and crackle to your tingling vocal vibrations.

142. *Fruit Heaven.* Arrive in the bedroom with two pieces of a soft, juicy fruit – mango, orange, papaya, tomato, or the like. (My personal favorite is the cherimoya. It has the texture of slightly gritty but firm custard, and a flavor somewhere between banana, papaya, and pineapple. It's rare, but worth the effort of finding.) Cut your fruit of choice into wedges and squeeze the juice all over his genitals. Siphon it off with your lips. Then chisel a hole in the other piece of fruit and set it atop his stalk like a cap. Squeeze and swivel it, licking off the juices that dribble down his shaft and onto his testicles. Yum!

143. If you are using condoms with your man (see Appendix), you might as well make it as sensual as possible. Pick up some of those fairly tasty mint or chocolate-flavored ones and learn the magical trick of applying one with your mouth. Unroll it a little first to make it more pliable; then re-roll. Put water-based lubrication on your lips and in the receptacle of the condom. Holding the condom between your puckered lips, set it atop his penis. Get the unrolling started by using your

tongue to push the edges down a little. Then, with lips covering teeth, push against the rim to unroll it as far down the shaft as you can. Slip your fingers in to complete the job. I recommend practicing on a banana till you get the hang of it; then you go, girl!

144. *Super Suction.* When you are all the way down on him, cover your teeth with your lips and slowly pull back up, sucking as hard as you can. At the tip, release your lips and your suction, then quickly clomp on at the base again to reprise the sensual sucking withdrawal. Repeat this over and over till madness ensues, or, as the Taoist masters suggest, alternate your sucking strokes with tongue nibbles on just the glans. Either way, he'll quickly be overcharged with desire.

145. His little bag of gems needs loving, too. The girls from the Japanese sex clubs said one of their sexiest secrets is to roll his balls gently in their hands while mouthing his Warrior Weapon. You can also encase them with your lips, keeping your hand on his shank, and softly circle the underside of the tender sac with your tongue. Try alternating globes in your mouth, with a few gentle nose nudges in between. This should make the loose skin tighten with ecstatic tension.

146. ***Double His Pleasure, Double Your Fun.*** Position yourself so your lips are at his crotch and your alluring crevice is in his direct line of sight. While enjoying the satin feel of him in your mouth, let your fingers slide all over your undulating mound, making you feel extra lusty. He gets the double pleasure of your intensified oral ministrations and the most erotic view in the world. You get the double fun of hot throbbing maleness on your tongue and the swelling and quivering of your own quim.

The Gag-and-Swallow Challenge

You can make your lover feel uniquely cherished, secure, and understood by deeply engulfing his male essence. But this powerful act of validation can prove somewhat daunting to accomplish.

- Here are a couple of tricks for stopping that nasty gag reflex. (1) Prior to insertion, tap your left temple with your fingers and say to yourself, 'I will not gag.' Then tap your right temple, saying, 'There is no reason for me to gag.' (2) Inhale through your nose as he enters your mouth. Exhale as you slide him in deep. Mysteriously, these techniques work. And he gets the rare treat of nestling in the small wet cave at the back of your throat and feeling the exquisite contractions of the muscles there. To say nothing of the psychological thrill of a deep-throating woman.

- To swallow or not to swallow? Because it is every man's fantasy and the ultimate act of acceptance and penis worship, I say yes (provided that you're sure of his sexual health). Cleopatra asserted her prodigious female power by taking the art of swallowing to a new level: hundreds of soldiers in one night, it is said. Many tribal peoples view semen as a sacred, curative elixir, and some West African women eagerly ingest it to obtain the hormone prostaglandin, thought to be a contraceptive. Try suggesting to your lover that he drink more water or pineapple juice, and eat cinnamon or celery so his come will be tasty to the last drop. This really does work, and the very idea that you've mentioned it will start his mind racing and virility swelling.

- Another swallowing trick is to smear his trembling, about-to-explode firecracker with chocolate, honey, or soft peanut butter. You'll hardly taste the difference. And if you let his liquid flow right past your tongue and directly down the hatch, your taste buds won't even be involved. If he can smoosh his nose and mouth all around in your pungent juices, you can swallow his. He'll adore you for it.

147. While he's coming, perform the butterfly technique, or simply swirl your tongue thirstily around at the very tip of his penis. Adds zillions of shivers to his climax.

148. To prolong his orgasm, squeeze the glans with your mouth every few seconds while he is contracting. He will beg to become your slave.

149. *Afterglow Fellatio.* After he has ejaculated, allow his spent organ to remain resting in the haven of your warm mouth. Let him drift off to dreamland with his manhood lovingly encased, protected, and owned by you.

part ii: the handmaid's tradition

A man's weapon of love holds certain secrets that can be coaxed out only with your hands. Having more flexibility and power than your lips, your fingers can more precisely control his pleasure and activate crucial hot spots (see 'Penis Reflexology,' opposite). If you keep this in mind while you massage his instrument, you will not only fulfill his wet dreams, you may succeed in excavating his true potential as a man.

Penis Reflexology

Similar to the foot, the penis is like a small map of the rest of the body, and stimulating certain points on it enlivens the corresponding parts of his body, heart, and mind. For instance, if you want to build trust between the two of you, try giving him regular prostate massage. Or soothe his sore throat and cough by concentrating your fingerwork on the coronal ridge, which will also encourage him to express his emotions more readily. Here are some other points on the penis and their corresponding physical and emotional areas:

Entire penis: physical, mental, and emotional center of his masculinity.

Perineum and prostate (in physical sensation, it's comparable to your G-spot): feet and base of torso; root of his virility; primal, earthy feelings; trust.

Testicles: sex organs; creativity; potency; ability to build.

Lower two-thirds of shaft: belly and muscles; foundation of his personal power; bold decisiveness; ability to shape the powerful forces of the world; how he thinks of himself.

Upper third of shaft: heart; love; sensitivity; how he feels about you.

Ridge up center from base to glans: spine; courage; loyalty.

Coronal ridge: throat; ability to express his thoughts and emotions; generosity.

Frenulum (small fold of skin between head and shaft; in physical sensation, it's comparable to your clitoris): third eye; vision; dreams; wisdom.

Glans: top of the cranium; inspiration; enlightenment; spiritual and physical ecstasy.

Slit in glans: the doorway to his heart; emotional ecstasy.

150. ***The Anointing.*** Your hands will perform a much deeper and more slippery erotic massage if you use oil – almond, olive, Kama Sutra, or long-lasting massage preparations. An elegant method is to pour the oil over the back of your hand and let it cascade down over his divine phallus. However you accomplish the process, venerate his organ with your hands and words. Ancient worshipers poured scented oil on icons they wished to honor; so you are not only lubricating him, you are anointing him with appreciation and paying homage to his fruitfulness and power.

151. *Circle of Heaven.* While he is still soft, hold the base of his stalk with one hand and place the flat, well-lubed palm of the other on his glans. Letting his flaccid member lie on his belly and pelvis, slide the whole thing clockwise until it is pointing straight down. There, encircle the shaft and stroke down. Flatten your palm again, and continue the clockwise circle, moving his organ up to the starting position. Repeat in continuous heavenly rounds. Penis Refloxology bonus: You are warming up his heart, fantasies, and ecstatic pathways.

152. *Basic Cobra.* Here's the classic stroke with some sexy refinements. Oil hands. Hold the base and/or scrotal sac with one hand, then cup the other like a cobra and cradle his upright arrow in it, closing the wrap with your thumb. Stroke up and down fluidly, and (1) flick your thumb across his frenulum as you pass by; (2) squeeze harder as you reach the top, tap the head with your thumb, release pressure or even open your hand on the way down; or (3) lightly press on testicles or perineum simultaneously. Penis Reflexology bonus: extra stimulation to his primal as well as lofty feeling centers.

153. *Juicing.* Holding the loose skin taut at the bottom, grasp his fruit of love in your other well-oiled hand and slide it upward. Squeeze as if you're juicing an orange, pulsing tighter and releasing several times all the way up. This will remind him of the hot contractions of your PC muscles when he is inside you.

154. *Twisting the Tiger.* Clasp his untamed animal with both hands, one stacked atop the other. Twist your lubricated hands in opposite directions as you glide up and down, varying speed and pressure. Lean your body forward and back in rhythm with your hand movements and purr with lust.

155. *Maestro.* Occasionally, take hold of his baton and tap the sensitive tip against your palm, breast, or pubis – or against his own belly – or back and forth *between* your two pelvises. Penis Reflexology bonus: You are inspiring and physically 'enlightening' him.

156. *Milking.* With one slippery hand, stroke from base to tip, sliding completely off the end, and immediately do the same with the other hand. Alternate upward flings in a smooth, continuous motion. He will feel as though he is continually emerging from your grasping love lips. Reverse the direction, milking downward, and he will feel as if he is repeatedly entering your velvet grotto.

157. ***Spreading Joy.*** Glide the heel of one well-oiled hand down from glans to base, as if you are petting a favorite cat. Keep this up as, with the other hand, you caress from thigh to belly to other thigh in one big arc, spreading erotic energy farther out from the center of his sex. You can also distribute the pleasure to his heart area by circling his nipples with your palm or fingertips. This is great for defusing sexual tension that may be about to explode, or for getting him used to the idea that there's more to eroticism than his penis.

158. ***The Rack.*** Grasp the bottom of his weapon with one lubricated hand and his jewel sac with the other, palms facing toward his body, and the thumb-sides of your hands together. Stretch your hands away from each other, stroking up the spine of his naughty tool with one and pulling down across his deliciously tortured testicles with the other. Penis Reflexology bonus: You are sending his male power up to the heart (along the central ridge of his penis, the location that corresponds to courage), as well as down to the source of his creative genius. He might think up new ways to love you fearlessly.

159. ***Tunnel of Love.*** Fold your well-oiled hands together, fingers interlocked and thumbs crossed. Then glide the womblike encasement of your clasped hands up and down his quivering limb. If you slightly tighten your index fingers and thumbs, and if you occasionally squeeze just like your PCs would, it will feel even more like the love tunnel he dreams about.

160. *Barefoot Butterfly.* As an occasional change of pace from sliding movements, press the tip of his love weapon gently against his belly with one hand while you flicker the backs of your other fingers teasingly up and down the shaft. Switching to the flat fronts of your fingers will make it feel as if the butterfly's feet are dancing across his delighted stalk as well.

161. *Praying for Fire.* Put the flats of your hands together as if in prayer. Then, inserting his stiff stalk between them, rub your hands back and forth as if trying to start a fire from twigs. Travel up and down along the sides, or point your fingers skyward and make fire along the front and back of his thunderbolt. Vary your speed, pressure, and placement, and every now and then slip the shaking glans in your mouth as you continue building his flame.

162. *Fingers Only.* Place his lance in the oiled crotch between your index and middle fingers (using either one or both hands) and stroke slowly up and down. Press your knuckle across the sensitive frenulum and slit in the glans with every few passes, and tighten or loosen your slender love vise depending on how deeply he moans. Penis Reflexology bonus: You are opening the door to the dreams of his heart.

163. *The Corkscrew.* With one hand, hold his penile skin taut at the base. Wrap your other lubricated hand, palm facing his belly, around the root of his stalk and slide upward. When you reach the glans, twist your hand around like you are turning a corkscrew, then open your palm and glide down the other side, or let your hand come off completely before returning to your starting position to repeat. Use a light touch; too much pressure will ruin the effect. For variety, you can hold his missile pointing down toward his feet, then stroke and twirl in a downward direction. Penis Reflexology bonus: You are encouraging him to express his power through generosity and wisdom.

164. *Reflexology Rubdown.* Give your lover's manhood a titillating massage that will also heal and harmonize his entire being. With well-lubricated hands, warm up his member by simply opening and closing your palms and fingers around it all the way up and down. Lay his penis on his belly and use flat hands to sweep across it in opposite directions, covering the entire length. Cup one hand around back and massage in small circles all the way up the central ridge (his 'spine') with either fingertips or thumb of the other hand. Gently cradle his testicles in your palm and lightly palpate the perineum, the very root of his primal manhood. Then knead, squeeze, and pet any other area on his penile body map that you particularly want to awaken.

Finish by enclosing his shaft between both curved palms and slowly gliding up and down, allowing the back of your bottom hand to caress and soothe his belly. Then hold his manly organ to your heart for a brief moment of loving connection.

the sum of the parts

At various points during any phallic massage, it can be especially effective to concentrate briefly on just one small section. Then continue your all-over stroking and perhaps return to that same area, or select a new one. This pinpoint lust-building can fill you with a sense of power, while his internal circuits will be sizzling hotter than usual. Use your intuition and the quality of his moans to determine where he would most appreciate your finely honed ministrations.

165. *Perineum.* As the exterior wall of his prostate, this area has been compared to your deeply sensitive G-spot. Use the heel or knuckles of one hand to vibrate there while you caress or simply hold his love wand. Or gently press in and out on the perineum with trance-inducing pulsations. Penis Reflexology bonus: activating his sexy virility and manly essence.

166. *Testicles.* Cradle his delicate bulbs in one hand, grasping their root between your

thumb and forefinger. Keep your other palm flat and circle it over the surface; lightly rake your fingernails in cunning designs; even place a full-lipped kiss there occasionally. Penis Reflexology bonus: maximizing his creative power and latent potency.

167. *Frenulum.* Grasp the base of his shaft firmly while you circle a thumb hypnotically over this super-sensitive spot, which is similar to your clitoris in its response to sensation. Alternatively, massage this small fold of skin delicately between your thumb and index finger, or use the heel of your hand, fingers extended over his tummy, to create circles of bliss that radiate out to the entire pelvic area. Penis Reflexology bonus: accessing his erotic dreams and visionary wisdom.

168. *Coronal ridge.* Holding his skin taut at the base, form a ring with your thumb and index finger and twist it around the shaft just where it joins the glans. Occasionally, bring this ring up and off the top of his throbbing organ. Penis Reflexology bonus: encouraging him to express his thoughts, feelings, and generosity.

169. *Glans.* Hold his weapon firmly upright and, with the palm of your other hand, inscribe small circles on the tip; smooth it side to side and up and down; and cup the palm to form a twisting and lifting cap. You can also place your fingertips over the head like a closed umbrella and

gently squeeze them up and off the tip. If he is uncircumcised, massage his glans first through the foreskin, then slowly slide it down to expose and caress the more sensitive skin beneath. Penis Reflexology bonus: Here's where you truly inspire him and bring him to ecstatic enlightenment.

170. *Slit in glans.* Cradling his lance in both hands, gently rub alternating thumbs up and down the slit. Very delicately slide your thumb into the crevice and pulse, then softly massage. Watch his face carefully for reactions to your pressure. Penis Reflexology bonus: Through this door to his heart, you are paving the way for love to flow freely.

special effects

171. *Gotcha Covered.* Instead of using oil, cover his magic wand with some thin, smooth fabric, rubbing it softly over his skin and massaging him right through that new texture – the bedsheet, a lacy camisole, your silky panties or stockings.

172. *Steam Room.* While you are massaging his weapon, keep your mouth near it so he can feel your hot panting breath steaming it up. And whenever it passes within reach, lick just the tip of it with your eager tongue.

173. ***The Full Nelson.*** Have him sit on the edge of the bed, facing a large mirror. You sit and straddle him from behind, your pubis pressed tight against his bottom, breasts leaning into his back. Slip your well-lubricated hands around to his chest, running your fingers over his nipples, belly, and finally down to his shivering erection. Squeeze his testicles, stroke his shaft, and writhe sensually against his back as he watches with delight in the mirror. When you really get into this, you may feel like his penis is attached to *your* body.

174. ***The Piston.*** When his missile is nicely erect, interrupt your sensual squeezes to make one quick stroke from bottom to top, and down again, like a piston. Continue massaging erotically for several breaths, then give him two fast piston strokes. Massage awhile; then do three quick up-and-down strokes. Continue increasing the number of piston strokes, with caressing pauses, until his engine has reached the boiling point. Then use only fast, tight pumping motions to drive him over the edge.

175. ***Slow Torture.*** Delay builds tension, excitement, and peak sensation, so as an occasional treat, try to keep him on the brink as long as possible. Caress him slowly and mercilessly with oiled hands until he is nearing orgasm. Then take your hands away completely and offer him your nipples to kiss. After he has calmed down sufficiently, resume your genital massage until he has neared his peak again. Then delay him with the squeeze technique (see page 77). Slowly bring him close to climax a third time, until he is almost shaking with sex, and then back away to rub your own breasts and moist furrow while he watches in divine agony. Take your time re-applying oil before approaching him yet again, this time caressing only his inner thighs and belly to spread some of his unbearable tension to other body parts. Stop and start him as many times as you think he can take it before finally stroking him to a shuddering, explosive orgasm.

176. *The Sacred Cream.* In a man's secret dreams, his woman treats the hot cascade of his orgasm not as a messy goo, but as a divine elixir – a golden potion only he can mix, the vital fluid that carries the essence of his manhood and his sacred seed. And that's exactly what it is. So when the desire you have built in him finally gushes out, ecstatically massage the heavenly fluid all over your thighs, belly, breasts, or face (it's actually a great, protein-rich skin cream). This artistic gesture of adoration will bind his heart to yours like nothing else can.

7

the back of beyond

I believe in the flesh

and the appetites . . .

and each part of me is

a miracle. Divine I am inside and out, and

I make holy whatever I touch or am touched from.

—Walt Whitman, Song of Myself

Honored by the ancients as a place of explosive and sacred sexual fire, that magnificent little bud nestled in your derriere is waiting to be rediscovered. No other spot can bring on the furious lust of an unleashed woman, or the deep erotic sensibilities of a man, quite like this one. Why? Because the anal cavity is richly lined with tons of sensitive nerve endings; because contracting the surrounding muscles stimulates a rush of sex hormones; and because an aroused bottom loosens and vitalizes the entire pelvic area, increasing sensitivity, movement, and orgasmic bliss.

For men, an eroticized posterior will help him control his ejaculatory power and open him to previously camouflaged emotions and sensitivities. Further, you can best stimulate one of his key erogenous zones, the prostate gland, from inside this modest little seat of pleasure.

In women, this rear tunnel lies next to the vaginal canal, and the sphincter is actually part of the web of sensitive clitoral and G-spot tissue. So stimulation of this rear grotto can provide a delicious new sense of fullness and ravishment as well as kindle an earthier, more primal internal fire. And because it feels tight, is rarely offered, and seems magnificently kinky, a woman's behind is the forbidden cavern of men's dreams.

If you think anal loving is dirty, think again. Unless you've had a recent bowel movement, the area should be clean and clear. If you have trepidations, then this is where your willingness to be outrageous and cross new sexual borders comes into play. If you think it's not fun, then you haven't tried it under the proper circumstances. With the right man, the right attitude, and the right lubrication, you can catapult both of you into a tantalizing realm of untapped sexual experience. So whip out your Passion Trigger of choice – how about a crease-stimulating G-string, a titillating sense of the taboo, a bout with the hula, or a mental picture of *The Last Tango in Paris* – and begin your love affair with this hotbed of earthy new delights.

Vital Keys to Back-Door Pleasure

Key #1: Lubricate. The anus has no lubrication of its own, so some sort of anointing is *required.* Saliva, vaginal fluids, or Astroglide will smooth the way gloriously.

Key #2: Arouse other areas first. A high level of arousal enlivens the posterior cave, making it *much* more receptive to touch. Trying to do it the other way around dooms you to failure. Keep up the genital caresses *during* anal stimulation, too; it comforts, distracts, and forges the entire pelvis and buttocks into one fiery furnace.

Key #3: Take it slow. The tortoise wins the race here. Even with a gentle, languid touch, it may take hours, weeks, or months for the shy and tender rear flower to relax and blossom fully. Be patient!

Key #4: Push out. When you are receiving back-door sex, completely relax, or push your anal muscles out as when you are having a bowel movement. Clenching causes unnecessary discomfort.

plucking his ripe apple

177. Often detailed in French erotica, a one-finger massage on the outer rim, or even just in front of it, right before he comes is a fabulous way to initiate your man into the deep eroticism of anal stimulation. But beware; this is likely to bring on immediate orgasm.

178. While you are titillating his pleasure stalk with your hand or mouth, slip one lubricated finger around back. Softly caress the rim of his anal apple until it relaxes enough for you to *gently* insert your fingertip. Vibrate your finger and make small circles, creeping ever-so-slowly deeper and deeper. As many times as necessary, pause and wait for him to loosen up, all the while maintaining your penis pleasuring. Once inserted, gently curve your finger up and down his inner walls, covering only about an inch of territory. Don't remove your dancing digit until he has exploded in ecstasy.

179. Adorn a finger with your recently stripped-off panties, moisten it with saliva, and

wetly circle the rim of his rear opening. Push your pantied fingertip inward and, as he begins to buck with excitement, leave the molded lingerie inside as you gently remove your finger. As you would do in the famous Oriental pearl technique, slowly pull your silks out at the moment of climax.

180. Dare to kiss his luscious bottom. Men never expect it and can hardly believe their stupendously good fortune. You can, of course, slather your tongue all over your guy's cute butt, but when you spread his cheeks and lap voraciously at the soft bud hidden there, he will really go ballistic. (Make sure he's clean first, of course!) Massage his overheated piston while you sculpt anal circles, draw vertical swaths up and down the crease, and make delicate wet insertions with your pointed tongue. Alternating this with love bites and tender smacks to his fleshy cheeks makes for a splendid contrast.

181. *Madam Pele's Prostate Massage.* Often compared to the G-spot, your man's prostate gland is one of his hottest arousal buttons. To reach it from inside, insert your lubed and manicured finger in very slow and gentle stages into the recesses of his tender bottom. When you are in as deeply as possible, crook your fingertip forward and you will make contact with a chestnutlike mound – his prostate. Vibrate, stroke, and zigzag across it, judging what pressure to use by his reactions. And always remember to keep

him secure in his masculinity by caressing his penis simultaneously. In fact, try pulsing against his prostate with your finger while you sweep downward on his missile with your other hand, so that the two strokes 'meet.' He'll feel as though the base of his penis and even his perineum are being surrounded by hot lava. Just watch out for violent eruptions!

electrifying your dark passage

Keeping in mind that fingers, tongues, and penises should never move directly from anus to vagina (the mix of internal cultures can cause infection), you and your man can delight in discovering a new erogenous zone that many women prefer above all others.

182. Introduce yourself to the earthy tingles of your own bottom by letting the hot shower water pour across your spread cheeks and into the satiny crevice. Massage your backside flower with one soapy hand while you rub vaginal lips and clitoris with the other. You may come to think of it as your second love bud.

183. *Aphrodite's Crease.* Like any great love goddess, Aphrodite understood that her gleaming orbs of flesh were a powerful

aphrodisiac. In one of her most famous statues, she is shown glancing over her shoulder to admire, and present to the world, her own beautifully undraped bottom. Your man will not be able to resist when you bend over and similarly offer him the velvety crease of your bottom. By pressing your lubed mounds together to construct a slippery tunnel for his rumbling train, you can create the illusion of full anal sex.

184. If you haven't tried cunnilingus from the rear, do so today. Your widely spread labial lips and the downward pull of gravity make for increased pressure and intensified sensations. And – you know where I'm going with this – you can then sweetly proffer the deep, intoxicating well of your behind to his tongue as well.

185. In the midst of hot coupling, guide his hands to your backside and encourage him to squeeze, slap, and pinch your cheeks. Then wriggle around so his fingers reach your anal rim and invite his caresses there with moans of delirious pleasure.

186. *Backseat Driver.* Many women are not crazy at first about the idea of anal sex, but when a man with a patient, magical, and slickly lubricated penis comes along to introduce them to the luscious feeling of fullness and top-notch G-spot stimulation, crossing this frontier can be a thrilling sexual epiphany. One woman I know was

so transported by her back-door discovery that she decided to take the helm. 'Soon,' she says, 'I was gleefully lowering my behind over his magnificent rod while we sat face-to-face in the backseat of his car – and I was having the ride of my young life!' Actually, this is quite a good position, as your legs have to be spread wide (opening and relaxing your inner burrow), and you can control all the driving action.

187. *Back-door Swing.* Oil his instrument and invite him to enter your rearside abyss from the doggie position. Make sure he proceeds slowly and tenderly, while you stroke your own pubis until you're loose and randy. Then reach back further to clasp his hanging balls. While you hold him quite still, sway your whole body back and forth over his delightedly captive weapon.

188. *Guinevere's Rump.* Sit on a pile of pillows or a low footstool, leaning back to prop yourself with hands on the floor. Command your well-lubed knight to kneel between your thighs and surrender his weapon into your rear antechamber. At this comfortable angle, you can both remain motionless while your anal muscles squeeze and pulsate around his lance, or you may permit him to swing his sword ecstatically in and out of your royal rear sheath. If you then raise your legs over his shoulders, you'll both be in Camelot.

189. *Around the World in Eighty Minutes.* Have him lie on his back while you pleasure him first with your French kisses, then with your wild African bush, and finally with your rear Lotus Blossom. If this lusty world travel doesn't drive him completely round the bend, I don't know what will.

8

secret erogenous zones

Cover me in mock hot breaths,

Surprise shivers up my spine

To cascade downward, then, in choruses of

Unseemly Noises and tummy trembles

Tiny nips and bites teaching new delights

And when I think it must be all done

Stun me weak with feather kisses blown

down my leg

Charming disarming me with delicious unpredictables

Invent me all over again . . .

—Marcia Singer, M.S.W., C.H.T.,

'Softplay Me'

While it's true that a man's erotic feelings are centered in the throbbing hub between his legs, it's your challenge as a virtuoso lover to awaken his body to fresher and more diverse delights. By helping him reenergize old familiar spots and develop previously undetected erogenous zones, you become the heroine of his erotic story. It's you who unlocks the door to the secret palaces he never knew he had; you who makes his orgasm a whole-body experience; and you who is forever associated with these new ecstasies in his erotic imagination and memory. Besides, there's no greater Passion Trigger than a secret spot on a man's arm or foot radiating new signals of desire to the woman who just gave it life.

190. *The Whole Ball of Wax.*

Reinvent your man's sensuality by eroticizing his entire body. Bring him to erection and then concentrate on other body parts, either maintaining constant penile contact with one hand, or returning there often between more far-flung destinations. If you have to bribe him to be patient with promises of hour-long oral sex or other favorite treats, do so. He'll soon figure out for himself that spreading his erotic feelings around builds up a much larger and deeper orgasmic charge. Use fingers, lips, or aromatic and stimulating massage oils to excite areas near his genitals and gradually creep out to his fingertips and toes. Or hold him in your mouth while you use fingertips to radiate hot energy outward, like spokes from a wheel hub. Yet another option is one of the most frequently requested activities in Japanese sex clubs – licking his *entire* body with your pointed tongue.

191. *The Magic Mouth.* You've been there, but have you done this? Kiss just the *inside* of his mouth, as if 'sucking the water of life.' Or take both of his lips between your own and play lip flute. Breathe hotly on his mouth, then lick or bite. Drink his saliva. Suckle at his tongue. Sip wine and then release it into his mouth through a deep kiss. Oriental love sages believe that there's a direct connection between a man's lower lip and his penis, so try shivering his timber with a fingernail scrape, love nibble, or sucking kiss to only the bottom half of his kisser.

192. *The Brazilian Kiss.* Come to bed clad only in a silk neck scarf. Place the corner of it in your mouth and, as you kiss him, thrust the fabric between his lips with your tongue. Suck it back into your mouth and rethrust it into his. As those lusty Latin women know, the wet silk traveling back and forth between your tongues awakens novel sensations that routine kisses have allowed to lie sleeping.

193. *The Upper Well of Desire.* The line of skin that goes from the top of his throat down to the soft well in the center of his

collarbone is analogous to the ridge down the middle of his member, ending in the dip of the scrotum. Suck teasingly and flick your tongue over this sensitive area, lapping for the milk of his desire in the tender depression at bottom.

194. *The 'Y'MCA.* There's something about a man's underarm – maybe the masculine aroma or the mixture of powerful biceps with tickling vulnerability – that brings out the tigress in me. You can ignite the manly erotic flames smoldering there by simply lifting his arm and petting him like a cat, sometimes just grazing the tips of his fur. You can scrape your nails softly down the hypersensitive center, or just snuggle your nose in and purr. Or use your tongue to circle the whole area, lap delicately across, or dip teasingly in and out of the deepest part.

195. *The Valley of Love.* Between the swells of his pecs lies an erotic ravine not normally explored. The skin here is thin and tender, and underneath it all lies the thymus gland, which regulates loving feelings. Drumming, tapping, circular rubbing, and tender kisses here induce trancelike states of open-hearted devotion and sensual bliss. A simultaneous lick to each nipple will usually produce shuddering sighs of ecstasy.

196. *Palming the Peak.* Another sexy arroyo is the very center of his palm. A small vein nestles quite close to the surface there and will

throb with the inrush of hot blood if you pulse insistently with your thumb or pointed tongue. Because the center of his palm has a nerve connection to the tip of his love weapon, your tingly messages will travel all the way up his arm and through his heart to the very summit of his manhood.

197. *The Sweet Spot.* The lower inside quadrant of each buttock is a soft, sensitive pleasure zone. During foreplay, oil your lips and glide them in mesmerizing figure eights over this sweet spot. When he is on top of you, grasp him there and squeeze forcefully in rhythm with his thrusts, or graze your fingernails across with increasing pressure as he nears what will now be an earth-moving climax.

His Secret Erection Center

Where it is: along the lower spine, between the tailbone and seven to nine inches above it.

What it is: a nerve complex that controls the rising of his love serpent.

What it does: increases erection power and strength; enhances the delicious swelling feeling he gets.

How to beckon its powers: strong, pulsing pressure with your whole hand; firm, circular rubbing with the fingertips; light to insistent stroking when he has begun to crest into orgasm.

Why it's magic: Because he has no idea what's going on or why he feels so kingly and potent, he will think you are some sort of shamanic snake charmer.

198. *Foot Telegrams.* A foot massage can open his whole body to yummy sensuality, but pressing certain foot reflexology points can produce even more erotic effects. Press with your fingertips and hold, or gently massage, the small cavity just below the ankle and beside the Achilles tendon to fire off messages to his penis. Nestle your thumb in the tender hollow just under the pad of his second toe (and next to the big toe pad) to open the floodgates of his heart. And palpate the middle of the fleshy ball of the foot to harmonize his unruly hormones with his feelings of higher love.

199. *The French Shrimp Job.* After a French Don Juan blew my friend Marianne's painted toenails off on a beach in Guadaloupe, she adapted this technique for use on her men. Lift his foot and dig your thumb into the cleavage between his first two toes. With your commanding thumb in place, stroke his foot as you gently rub the sole against your hot cheek. Run your tongue along his instep; kiss and make love to every curve. Separate his big toe from the others and suck it as if it were his swollen love organ, swirling your

tongue all around it and occasionally looking up archly into his eyes. Duplicate these efforts on each toe, and end by caressing his foot tenderly and bringing it to your nurturing breast. Something about the combination of being manhandled as well as worshiped works to make an entirely new erogenous zone of his foot, and a hot thunderbolt of his love weapon.

200. *Testosterone City.* Because they are so often neglected in loveplay, a man's testicles are a rich source of undiscovered pleasure. The skin covering them is thinner and contains less fat than elsewhere, and the bags inside produce 95 percent of his testosterone; so they are the source of his manhood, yet one of the most sensitive spots on his body. The operative idea here is snuggle, not juggle. Lick them, kiss them, suck them gently into your mouth. Cradle them in your hand, and lightly caress just the bottom of the sac (if you concurrently look deeply into his eyes and tell him you adore him, his heart will be yours). During intercourse, reach back and stroke them or delicately push them up toward his thrusting sword. Treasure them like jewels and he'll have a new appreciation of you as a wise and deeply sexy woman.

The Male G-spot

What it is: The prostate (which originates from the same embryonic tissue as your G-spot does) is a walnut-size gland that lies between his rectal cavity, his bladder, and the root of his penis. Accessible from the perineum (a spot midway between his testicles and anus) or from inside the anal cavity, it is considered the great unexplored wilderness of a man's sexuality.

What it does: During arousal, the prostate swells with seminal fluid and becomes exquisitely sensitive. During orgasm, it spasms in order to propel semen through his love pump, providing that divine feeling of orgasmic inevitability.

What to do with it: While sucking or massaging his fleshy spear, press firmly into the perineum with your manicured fingertips or the flat part of your knuckles. Send vibrating tremors deep inside by shaking your fingers or by pulsing rhythmically in and out. Or you can simply stroke the area up and down or in hypnotic circles. When he's inside your love nest, try reaching around to palpate just behind his testicles – this will swell his penis even more and prolong his on-the-edge arousal. An age-old trick used by Oriental courtesans to assure repeat business was to press the perineum firmly *during* climax, thereby drawing out and enhancing his orgasmic ecstasy. Even if your man's G-spot isn't particularly responsive at first, your regular perineal massage will gradually intensify his sensitivity and transform this hidden gold mine into one of his favorite erogenous zones. (For stimulation of the prostate through his back door, see chapter 7.)

the triads of desire

When your lover kisses you, you feel a warm, flooding tingle not just on your lips, but also in your breast, your womb, and sometimes even in the bottoms of your feet. That's because there's an internal circuit of nerves and biomagnetic energy that links all the main erogenous zones with one another and connects them to the brain. Stroking one stimulates another, like when he pinches your nipple and you feel a hot surge in your clitoris. According to ancient love sages, certain combinations of erotic points are more potent than others, forming highly charged Triads of Desire. Simultaneously stimulating all three points of any triad will strengthen their electric connection and build heat, trembling desire, and orgasmic tension throughout the entire body.

201. *The Lip Nipple Triad.* Simultaneously stimulating the two nipples and the mouth creates dynamic sexual energy in the upper body, in contrast to the arousal usually

concentrated only in his genitals. Suck on his lips while insistently kneading both nipples. You will make his breathing deepen, his mouth water, and his shoulders tremble, while flooding his head with intoxicating heat. Watch his missile of love rise in a passionate arc that involves his whole body.

202. *The Nipple Root Triad.* Connecting the two nipples and the penis, this triangle greatly intensifies the euphoric quality of ordinary genital sensation. Lick his shaft while gently twisting his nipples, or nibble at one berry while you massage his shivering member and other nipple with your hands. This forms a vortex of hot rapture that undulates throughout his pelvis, spine, and heart. (You can also set your nipples and pelvic mound against his and wriggle atop him.) The addition of the second nipple combined with genital stimulation carries his erotic tension over the top into a tidal wave of almost unbearable bliss.

203. *The Phallic Foot Triad.* Activating this triangle, which links the penis with the nerves in the bottom of the feet, creates the feeling of delicious confinement while fiery sensations circulate throughout his entire lower body. Cradle his feet while giving him magnificent oral sex. Suck and massage all his toes while using your foot to tweedle his genitals. Or simply trail your fingertips across his throbbing member and

down his inner thighs and calves to his instep. Because of the foot reflexology points, you will also be connecting his sexual power with his head and heart.

204. *The Supernova.* Combine the Lip Nipple Triad with the Nipple Root Triad to multiply their mind-blowing power. When your genitals are thrusting together in love, pause a few moments to imagine the electric pathway between these four points. Then bring your mouth close to his as you twist both his nipples between your fingertips, just enough to create a noticeable surge in his throbbing missile. Resume thrusting as you probe his mouth with your tongue and tune the frequency arcing through his nipples like a human radio. You can also activate this diamond while engaged in mutual oral sex by simply pinching his nipples. When you ignite all the main erotic points at once, you create an intense fire throughout his entire body, mind, and soul. Make sure he's prepared to withstand the heat.

9

s and 'mmmm'

After a night and day of love,

Krishna and Radha lay down to sleep . . .

Marks of her teeth were on his shoulders.

Marks of her nails were on his back.

His body was bruised with her passionate
embraces.

A god wears the signs of those who love him.

—*Surdas*

My version of S&M has nothing to do with pain or humiliation and everything to do with intensifying pleasurable sensations. It's electric, fun, and very intimate – something that lures you and your lover just slightly over the edge of your usual boundaries. While having nails scraped down your back may sound unpleasant, during flame-hot lovemaking, it can feel deliciously intense. So, in the heat of passion, what was once a nibble can deepen into a bite. A loving tap can turn into a playful spank. A silk scarf may become a bond of love. And your ordinary roll in the hay can become a super-charged event that takes you both to the heights of erotic tension – or simply tickles your taboo button with some kinky loveplay.

The exchange of power and intimate vulnerability has been a natural part of lovemaking since the beginning of time. More recently, films like *9½ Weeks, Swept Away, Bound, Exit to Eden,* and *Quills* have enlightened even the most naive among us about the delectability of the dance of physical restraint and surrender. And we modern women are now hungry for the aphrodisiac of wielding some sexual power – whether it comes from enthralling or being enthralled by someone you love. After all, who doesn't long to be gloriously stung by pleasure?

No need to cast about for Passion Triggers here. Between blindfolds, fur-lined handcuffs, leather outfits, and fantasies of erotic command, there are plenty to burn. So throw off the shackles of convention. Take sword in hand, Mistress, and rattle your slave's cage today!

Safety First

- Play at surrendering, or being surrendered to, only with someone you *trust*.
- Play only within your comfort zone. Be honest and forthcoming about what feels good, what feels marginal or scary, and what hurts.
- Test toys on yourself first. That paddle may not feel as soft, or as hard, as you think.
- For more serious scenes, negotiate beforehand. 'I am willing to be the naughty schoolgirl and get spanked, but I also want lots of praise and kissing.' Or 'When I take you prisoner, are there any ways you would prefer I *not* punish you?'
- Never combine intoxicants with powerplay; you tend to overlook important signals.
- Use 'safe words.' You need to know when he's begging for mercy because he loves it or because he really wants you to stop. Common ones are 'yellow light' for 'Wait. It's almost too much. Let's talk,' and 'red light' for 'STOP EVERYTHING RIGHT NOW!'

- For bondage games (1) never put pressure on throat, hands, joints, armpits, or creases of the crotch; (2) never leave a restrained person alone for more than a few seconds; (3) always have scissors available that will cut through the restraints in case of emergency; (4) always have soothing ointments, chocolate treats, and words of love ready for the 'de-bonding.'

initiating your man

205. Try gently pounding on his back or chest during your orgasm. In your excitement, you just couldn't help it. Or give him one good swat on the behind when he's coming, just trying to 'bring his thrusts in deeper.'

206. Present your lover with a card that says, 'This entitles the bearer to the services of one Slave of Love for the weekend.' Sign your slave name to it – for example, 'Veronica the Vassal.'

207. Hand him several of his old ties and ask him to tie you to the bed until you've had three orgasms.

208. Wear one piece of leather clothing to bed – gloves, vest, spiky heels, short skirt, corset, panties, bra, belt. The feel, look, and smell of leather are likely to bring out a little kink in both of you.

209. Kneel before him, bare-breasted, to kiss and lick his feet. Caress his shins with your nipples as you croon submissively, 'How may I serve you, my king?'

210. Nipple clamps, when lightly applied, give you a titillating feeling of urgent pressure. And to him, they look deadly. Put some on and ask him to lick your nipples and/or your vulva until you beg for mercy.

211. As you undress him, slowly unbuckle his belt, then suddenly slash it off. Holding it at both ends, snap it a few times as you arch your eyebrow at him. Push him onto the bed, straddle him, and hold his chest down on the bed with his belt. Rub your pelvis against his. Keeping him pinned with your legs, suddenly unzip him, pull out his erection, and manhandle it. Immobilize him even further by tightening his trousers around his thighs, perhaps skimming his belt across his now-aching appendage. Suck, lick, and bite to your heart's content.

power games

212. *Paper, Scissors, Rock.* Challenge him to this simple hand game. When you win, whip out some real scissors, cut the clothes off his body, and ravish him.

213. ***Offtrack Betting.*** Make a bet with your guy over a sporting event. Whoever loses (which you can manage to do without too much trouble) has to go naked or wear a costume of the winner's choice for the rest of the day, night, or weekend and submit to any and all love commands. Have a *great* costume ready.

214. ***Pudding Torture.*** Slip a note into his briefcase that reads, 'Tonight, come home and get in bed naked. If you are a good boy, stay still, and don't come till I say you can, I promise to make it worth your while.' When he's abed, enter naked, carrying a bowl of warm pudding. Apply it to yourself provocatively, then lie atop him and squiggle. Lick the delicious glop off his nipples and erection, massage your own gooey breasts and bush, and screw his brains out, all the while commanding him to lie still and reminding him, 'Don't come till I tell you to.' Make him take it for a couple hours before giving him permission to ejaculate, any way you want him to.

215. ***Duchess for a Day.*** When it's you who wins the love bet, he is yours to command for the duration. You may want to garb your naked slave in a tie – to symbolize his servitude and to provide something for you to lead him around with on occasion. You might order him to prepare a candlelit bubble bath for you, scrub your back, and serve you dessert or champagne in the tub. Perhaps you'd like him to paint your toenails, massage your feet, or lick your breasts for one full hour. If he does a good job with these chores, reward him with kisses and well-placed caresses, keeping him in a state of semi-arousal. If he falls short of perfection, a playful spank to the rear or the penis should remind him who's boss. If you feel benevolent, allow him to have the pleasure of your velvety vulva around his slavish sword.

216. *Hell's Angel.* Every woman has a pet fantasy about being ravished, and within the bounds of consensual loveplay, it can be sexual dynamite to act it out. Attire yourself in rippable clothes and panties, put on an appropriate CD, and hand your ransacking hellion a motorcycle jacket. Let him chase you around the house before capturing you, tearing your clothes off, and spearing you over the top of a chair while you scream bloody murder.

217. *Command Performance.* Slip on the role of Mistress Marilyn along with your push-up bra, shiny thigh boots, and arm-length leather gloves. Invite him to perform oral sex on you or else. Then use this opportunity to teach him *exactly* how you like it done, instructing him on speed, placement, and technique. Good work deserves a reward.

218. *Mental S&M.* The dominance and submission game doesn't always have to involve leather, bondage, or harsh commands. Sometimes

slipping on a lacy camisole and asking your man to lie perfectly still while you read him some blazing erotica, or you share your kinkiest fantasies with each other, can provide just the right touch of delicious restraint. Perhaps make a rule that only you can do any touching, or vice versa. Tell him, 'If you forget to keep your hands to yourself, I shall have to use handcuffs.' Or maybe, as you're talking sex, lightly massage his aching member with a piece of fur – but go no further, no matter how much he wants it.

219. *Official Uniform.* Another way to lend an air of sexy dominance without really doing anything aggressive is to attire yourself in official dominatrix mufti. Don a pretty mask (maybe a feathered one), fishnet stockings, and carry a blindfold. Or clad yourself in a dark, tailored suit (without a blouse), slicked-back hair, and four-inch court shoes. Dress only in searing red lipstick, outlined in black lip liner. Perhaps wear a leather bra to bed. Sashay around, dressed in this manner, and, believe me, he'll take it from there.

blindfolds – an epicurean delight

Wearing a blindfold puts you in another world – private yet exposed, deprived yet sensorily enhanced. For men, who are particularly visual creatures, it can be exquisitely disconcerting.

Sex-toy stores carry a wide variety of blindfolds, including fur or fleece-lined, but satin 'sleep masks' are just as effective. A silk or cotton scarf makes a sensual sight-block, but the kinkiest of all is a pair of your own panties – what they lack in opacity, they make up for in psychological thrill and scent. Whether you shop for the perfect mask together or spring it on your man unawares, the slightly kinky aura of a blindfold will light deep inner fires.

220. A trick cleverly employed by some professional dominatrixes is to blindfold (and perhaps tie up) a man *before* she disrobes. That way he knows, and can feel, that she's naked; but not being able to actually *see* her exposed flesh drives him deliciously crazy.

221. Blindfold him. Then tease his flesh with your fingers, breath, hair, nipples, tongue, eyelashes, and pubic fur. Pause. Then suddenly thrust him into your moist vagina or eager mouth.

222. Bring his nerve endings close to the surface by exposing your blindfolded man to alternating tastes, textures, and smells. Rub him with an ice cube, then with warm honey. Feed him juicy fruit, crunchy nuts, creamy pudding or ice cream, tingly champagne. Massage him with fur or suede, tickle him with a feather, scratch him with a loofah or hairbrush. Offer him a whiff of vanilla food flavoring, the zest of an orange, a scented massage

oil, and the feel and aroma of your lingerie. Lick and kiss his rump, then give it a startling love spank.

Powerplay Roles

Costumes and role-playing are perfect for 'S and Mmmm.' Make your acts as serious as a religious ritual or as light as a Seinfeld comedy routine. Switch roles occasionally. Laugh, play, shock yourselves with kink. Bottom line: Play fair, play safe, play nice.

Roles	Props
• Amazon warrior and sex slave	Xena attire, rustic slave collar, whip
• Fierce pirate and ravishee	Bandanna, rubber sword, rippable clothes, swash-buckling music
• Nurse Ratchet and patient	White dress and stockings, antiseptic, tongue depressors
• French maid and randy master	Frilly apron, garters, lace restraints
• Schoolteacher and naughty student	Small eyeglasses, prim clothes, ruler
• Spanish Inquisitor and infidel	Long robe, shackles, Gregorian chant
• Rich bitch and pet dog	Mink, heels, dog collar

• Cop and interrogatee	Cap, badge, bright bare light
• Army captain and captured secret agent	Helmet, military jacket, handcuffs, marching music
• Countess and chauffeur	Jewelry, cigarette holder, peaked cap
• Lion tamer and lion	Safari shirt, high boots, whip, circus music
• Debutante and blackmailer	Prom dress, long gloves, play money
• Queen of female-only island and captured male invader	Sarong, crown, drums, Indy Jones attire
• Horse and rider	Reins, cowboy boots, country music

223. Having oral sex when you can't see is a completely different experience. Blindfold him and suck on his love weapon for at least thirty minutes. He will experience sensations he never knew existed.

sensual spanking

Spanking is hot. I don't mean the shaming, angry kind that hurts. I mean the kind where, in the middle of feverish sex, a lover administers a few sharp, sweet shocks of pleasure to skin that is flushed, vibrating, and craving deeper, more intense sensation. The *Kama Sutra* includes an entire chapter on the art of 'exchanging blows' as a highly erotic pleasure. It sets nerve endings atingle and cracks open your lovemaking into new levels of abandon and passion. Try it; you'll both like it.

224. *How to spank sensuously.* Start by running your fingers caressingly over his rump. Cup your hand slightly, keeping your fingers together. Then spank in a slightly upward direction, which produces more pleasure than a downward stroke. If you let your hand rest after landing a stroke and massage the spot briefly, it provides a warm, soothing contrast. The best place to attack is his 'sweet spot,' the lower, inner fourth of each cheek, but you can also give occasional exciting taps to his upper back or other very fleshy or very muscular areas (stay away from places where the bone is close to the skin). Whether you apply just one or several love swats, do it in the heat of passionate lovemaking, when the threshold between pain and pleasure has moved up quite a few notches, and your strokes will be welcomed and encouraged, not resented.

225. Wear leather or velvet gloves to bed. When you apply a love buffet in the ferocity of sexual madness, it will feel less sharp – smoother, richer, more sensual.

226. 'Whip' him with a feather, a pillow, or your panties.

227. According to Tantra, gentle blows on the nipples and perineum are excellent ways to start a burning fire in his loins. Try light taps with a closed fist or gentle flicks of the finger on these highly erogenous zones.

228. Caress or lick his throbbing member at the same time you are love-smacking his behind.

229. Try contrasting a stinging swat with the massaging of a vibrator.

230. While you are both thrusting lustily in the doggie position, moan or yell out, 'Spank me, you sexy brute!' After all, you're carried away by his overpowering, hot manliness.

231. Send electric messages to his brain by lightly spanking his proud penis. Hold the glans against his stomach with one hand, and cuff the shaft gently with the other. Flick your fingers quickly up and down his bulge, being careful to stay away from the too-tender tip. Shake, squeeze, and slap it lightly. Expect him to shudder with ecstasy.

232. When you are on the plateau near or

after climax, and your vaginal lips are engorged and pulsing, ask him to thump against your vulva with his throbbing weapon. It may even take you over the orgasmic brink.

the bonds of love

Many powerful men yearn to relinquish control to a thrilling woman, and to experience a delicious contrast to the decisive command they must display in their professional lives. In fact, being bound is one of the favorite requests men make of call girls – it's something exotic they doesn't usually get at home. It is not meant to overcome a man's reluctance, but to heighten erotic tension. The very idea that you can't escape from some very powerful sensations is extremely titillating and forces your body to ratchet up its pleasure receptors. Besides, bondage usually stretches or exposes the skin, which intensifies its sensitivity. As long as you trust each other and play intelligently (see 'Safety First,' page 127), a little friendly tying will add edginess and adrenaline to your lovemaking repertoire.

233. *Pretend bondage.* You may want to slide slowly into the idea of bondage by arranging your man in a somewhat helpless position, like having him lie atop his hands, and then instructing him to remain there *as if* he were tied. Challenge

his concentration by tickling him or giving him mind-blowing oral sex.

234. A little light bondage can be easily accomplished by using a silky scarf, a soft sash, or a piece of your lingerie to tie his hands to the bedpost. Then tell him an outrageous fantasy while you caress him with leather, fur, or scented oil. Scrape your nails lightly over his back and derriere, and fondle the golden scepter he has momentarily surrendered to you.

235. *Taste treats.* Use Velcro hand ties to bind your victim to the upper corners of the bed. Break out some really fine wine, dip your finger in the glass, and slide it across his lips. Dip in again, then glide it over his chest. Lovingly anoint other body parts. Follow this up by dipping your fingers into your own natural juices and lightly touching them to his upper lip.

236. Whip out your fur-lined handcuffs, perhaps just after he's arrived home, and shackle him, sitting, to the front door. Then 'desert' him and go change into something sexy, like a black Merry Widow, garters, and spike heels, while he's alone anticipating. (Don't be gone more than one or two minutes. See 'Safety First,' page 127.) Sashay right up to him and offer your exposed vulva to his lips. After you're satisfied, suddenly walk away again, leaving him to simmer in the fires of his lust and your musky aroma. Return in

a nurse's or French maid's uniform, unzip his trousers, and inspect him with your hands, breasts, and lips. Leave and return in various costumes, offering different parts of yourself to him and commanding the stop-and-go of his excitement, until fever pitch is achieved.

237. *Invigoration.* Have him lie face-down on the bed and, using rolls of gauze, tie his hands together at the top of the bed, and his feet together at the bottom. With the side of your fists and the cupped palms of your hands, pound and slap him all over, alternating the pressure between light and heavy and occasionally scraping your nails over his enlivened skin. Because of the way you've tied him, you should be able to easily turn him over to give him the same treatment on his front side. Invigorate him with all-over pinching, pounding, and flicking. Then bring out your scissors, perhaps running the cool steel over his hot flesh with an evil gleam in your eye, and cut him free of his bonds so he can 'retaliate.'

238. *Ride 'em, Cowgirl!* Purchase some 100 percent cotton rope in a hardware shop, and one evening when he least expects it, lasso him and tie him to the bed, hands apart, feet together. In your cowboy outfit (or perhaps just boots and bandanna), tease, rein, and tickle him mercilessly, finally hopping on top to ride him to that orgasmic pasture in the sky.

Tips for Tying

- Soften cotton rope by laundering it with fabric softener. Then cut it into several six-foot and twelve-foot lengths.
- To tie his wrists or ankles to bedposts, begin at the rope's midpoint and wrap it several times around the limb, finishing off with a square knot. Then tie the whole package to the bedpost.
- Having him wear boots, socks, or gloves will protect delicate skin and add a kinky aesthetic.
- To tie his hands behind his back, place his wrists one above the other in the small of his back (so he can lie comfortably on them). Slide the midpoint of the rope under his wrists, then bring the ends around his wrists and through the midpoint loop. Wrap each end in opposite directions between his wrists and tie with a square knot.
- An ordinary bow (or half-bow) makes a secure and easy-to-release knot. Make it your knot of choice whenever possible.

239. ***Sandwich Wrap.*** Wrap yourself tightly in cling film so that your nipples strain against the sheer bonds. Invite your lover to

unwrap you slowly, tie your hands behind your back with cling film, and eat you up.

240. *Silk Stockings I.* Dressed in bikini panties and thigh-high stockings, tell him that if he follows all your instructions, you'll give him a reward he'll never forget. Have him lie on the bed, holding his inner wrists against his outer thighs. Slip your stockings off provocatively and tie them around each of his arms and thighs together, finishing with an easy-release knot (a very comfortable yet helpless bondage position). Fondle him to erection. Then 'torture' him by ignoring the throbbing appendage and instead kneel over his face. Lock your thighs around his neck and press your bikinied love nest to his lips. When they are thoroughly moistened from his licking, slide your panties off, lay them across his face, and bid him to continue his wet ministrations. If he pleases you, reward him as desired.

241. *Silk Stockings II.* Wrap one of your black, seamed stockings several times around the base of his erect missile and pull the ends crosswise to tighten. Tie in a bow. Rub the silky ends against his testicles and lick his jewels right through the stockings while you massage his bound and swollen member. You may want to spank the impertinent thing as well.

242. *Silk Stockings III.* Wrap one stocking about halfway up his sword, leaving both ends untied. Lick, suck, and use your butterfly tongue to bring him near to explosion several times while you tighten and release the pressure of the wrapped stocking at will. Finally, whip off the silky binding just as he erupts like a hot volcano.

243. His old cotton socks, cut in long lengthwise strips, make excellent bondage ties. Truss his hands behind his back, sit him in a corner, and treat him to a sultry strip-and-dance routine. With his hands behind him, he won't be able to assuage his own ache – while you, on the other hand, can make him watch while you seductively tantalize yourself to a ferocious orgasm.

244. *Tied Up in a Meeting.* Pull out your rolling desk chair and ready some velvet cording. (If you can get away with this naughty trick behind the locked doors of his office, all the better.) Invite him to sit in the chair, and bind his hands behind the back of it. The skin of his nipples will be slightly stretched, so lick, tease, and bite them without mercy. Sit on the desk, spread your legs, and open your skirt just enough to give him a glimpse of your coral opening. Command him to roll the chair close and give you one lick only. Tease his body some more, alternating with proffered licks of your succulent furrow and tempting round bottom, until you finally deign to

sit atop his lap and screw his overworked brains out.

245. You can stiffen his organ quite magnificently just by presenting your bound breasts to him. Most women say they enjoy this tight sensation tremendously because it feels like having your full orbs squeezed by a lover. At the very least, the increased pressure will make your nipples bloom voluptuously and become exquisitively sensitive. You can find all sorts of alluring leather and chain 'bras' for this purpose in sex-toy stores, or you could cut out the cups of a regular bra that's several sizes too small. More seductive yet, offer several long silk scarves to your 'master' and ask him to tie them tightly around the top of your chest. He will gape in awed lust at the sight of your distended globes and the idea that you are bound for his pleasure.

246. Perhaps garbed as a severe schoolmarm, bend your naughty little boy facedown over the back of a chair and tie his hands to the arms with cotton shoelaces. Warm up his bare bottom with kisses and caresses before spanking it playfully with a Ping-Pong bat, hairbrush, or wide ruler. Pause to kiss his behind, massage his penis, and coo instructions about how you'd like his behavior to improve, before administering a few more sensuous whacks. The more aroused he becomes, the harder he'll want to be 'punished.'

247. *Secrets of the Orient.* American GIs were known to pay exorbitant prices for this delectable Oriental specialty. Tie his crossed ankles with thick yarn and have him lie on his back with legs bent. Sit on his chest (facing his feet) and circle his Jade Stalk with whipped cream from base to tip. Pin down his open legs by leaning on them with your arms as you envelop his quivering cock with your mouth. Lick and suck voraciously, until, just as he begins to climax, you remove your lips and cut off the restricting yarn with a sharp blade.

248. *Wet Bondage.* Attack where he leasts expects it – in his morning shower. Tie his hands to the nozzle and spank, slap, and scrape your nails over his soapy skin as water pours hotly over him – unless, of course, you want to shock him with a few blasts of cold water, too.

249. *Hair Band-age.* When he is fully erect, encircle his 'ponytail' with six of your scrunchies. Start at the bottom and smooth them on snugly. Then attempt to remove each one in reverse order, with only your lips, tongue, and teeth. Your wet efforts will drive him delightfully crazy, while the constriction of the bands delay his bursting orgasm until you've slipped off the very last one.

250. Leave a bag on his pillow that contains an outlined passage from *The Story of O* or

Anne Rice's (writing as A. N. Roquelaure) *The Claiming of Sleeping Beauty,* and all the equipment and costumes needed to reenact a scene of delicious bondage on you.

251. *Bedsheets from Hell.* Available from sex-toy catalogs, these fitted sheets have Velcro ties sewn onto them in perfect locations for spread-eagle hand and foot bondage. Surprise him one night by innocently throwing back the covers to reveal these suggestively kinky bed-trappings, and flip a coin to see who will be the binder and who the bindee.

252. *Japanese Massage.* Tie his hands and feet so that he's completely motionless and helpless. Use your hands, tongue, breasts, and saucy snatch to keep both his mouth and penis simultaneously stimulated. Then straddle his chest, facing his feet, and grasp the base of his now-flaming sword with one hand, pulling the loose skin down tight. Use your other well-lubricated hand to apply a series of quick upward strokes, about one per second. After fifteen of these, change to seven very quick, sharp strokes. Then fifteen slow ones again. Keep this up until he is near orgasm, apply the squeeze technique to temporarily delay him, and wriggle your glistening bush on his torso while you wait. When he has calmed down sufficiently, repeat the stroke series, squeeze technique, and wriggle. Bring him to the brink at least three times

before finally putting him out of his glorious misery.

253. *Taming the Tiger.* Every once in a while, it's fun to bind that unruly wild animal he carries around in his pants. It makes him feel deliciously constricted, sensitized, and owned by you. The easiest way to do this is with a leather cock strap, a quarter-inch-wide strip of leather that's six to ten inches long and has inside snaps to adjust the compression. Wrap it around the base of his flaccid member (or around both penis and testicles) and snap snugly. As he becomes erect, the binding grows tighter, so be careful not to over-torque. With well-lubed hands, stroke, drum, pinch, slap, and even bite that ferocious tiger – he will purr to stronger sensations now. Pluck at his pubic hair, and flick your fingers with a sharp snap on his swollen shaft. You should undo or reposition the strap after about fifteen to twenty minutes so as not to interfere with circulation, but you can leave it on until after orgasm. If you prefer, you can bind him with a tie, scarf, G-string, or cling film – just be sure it's quickly and easily removable or cutable. Your tiger will be roaring with excitement.

254. *Clip-ons for Him.* Tie your guy spread-eagled to the coffee table or dining-room table and apply a few titillating clamps. First test a nipple clip or ordinary wooden clothes-peg on the skin between your own thumb and forefinger (or nipple) so you get the idea just how powerful the

sensation is during and after being clamped. When he is highly aroused, try lightly clipping his belly button, earlobes, the base of his nipples, or the loose skin of his penis or balls. Lick but don't rub or pull. Pleasure him in other places, too. Don't leave clamps on for more than five minutes, and remove them slowly and gently because the blood rushing back in can hurt more than the clamping itself. If he likes the intensity of compression, he'll love these exhilarating tweakers.

leaving love marks

According to the *Kama Sutra,* the marks that lovers make on each other are sacred tokens of affection that when admired later, renew and rekindle their ecstatic love. These artful remembrances can be especially potent when left just before you are going to be separated for a few days or weeks.

255. ***Nail Marking.*** In the deep throes of passion, when the pain of a scratch becomes an exquisite pleasure, rake your nails deeply across his back, shoulders, arms, or rump, creating a straight or slightly curved 'Tiger's Tail.' Leave an even more artistic design by pressing your nails straight down into the skin, creating little half-moons all around his nipple (the 'Peacock's Foot') or just one small crescent on his hip (the 'New Moon'). He will be proud to know he has such a tigress for a lover.

256. *Biting.* While in the hot embrace of sex, clomp your teeth onto your man's shoulder or upper arm, mauling him like a lion and leaving random markings. When you want to be more artistic, sit on his chest, pull his head back by the hair, and create one 'coral jewel' or a whole 'necklace of gems' around his neck by squeezing the same spot several times between top teeth and lower lip. A low growl while administering these bites will add immeasurably to the erotic effect.

257. *Vampire Love.* Give him a good old-fashioned lovebite, but in an unusual place where only he can see the telltale bruise – next to his nipple or on his tender inner thigh.

afterplay

After the intensity and edginess of 'S and Mmmm' play, it's essential to create a reassuring, loving reentry to your everyday lives. Take off any costumes and resume your usual roles as husband and wife or warm lovers. Snuggle, kiss and hug, perhaps have cuddly regular intercourse. Pamper him with a scented bath, his favorite home-cooked meal, a long sensual massage, or an evening at the movies. Or simply offer him refreshments and drinking water while you chat caringly about what you both did and didn't enjoy. Explain to him that Mistresses need special coddling, too, and be ready with a suggestion for a loving service or gift he could provide to make you feel like an adored queen. These special and loving treats will encourage both of you to come back for more and make imaginative contributions for next time.

10

rapturous rituals

The venue of sex may have a hole in it. We slip out of the time and space of our lives and enter the theatrical milieu of the soul.

—*Thomas Moore,*
The Soul of Sex

Love beds are altars. People are temples encountering temples, the holy of holies receiving the holy of holies.

—*Matthew Fox,*
The Coming of the Cosmic Christ

Through lovemaking we often enter another reality, a borderland where we shed some of the conventions of everyday life to speak and act in ways otherwise unimaginable. Sometimes we even fall into altered states of consciousness or stumble upon a new self-discovery. But by organizing the raw energy of sex into a ritual, we become true magicians of love, endowing each kiss, glance, and thrust with a deliberate and elevated significance.

Whether it's as simple as lighting a few candles or as elaborate as a three-hour ceremony with costumes and anointings, a ritual gives our love-making a framework that sets it apart from ordinary reality and frees us to be as divine or as ribald as we dare. In this otherworldly domain, sexual intimacy becomes high art, and communication becomes soulful communion.

How to Concoct a Ritual

Making sex into something deeper and more profound can take some extra time and thought. But the careful preparations, accoutrements, and acts of ritual are Passion Triggers that invite the Dionysian deities of love into your bedroom and imbue all your actions with original magic. Always include all three of these ingredients in your alchemical brew.

Ingredient #1: Preparation.

Intention transforms the ordinary into the sublime. So consciously decide to let the sex act become a meaningful rite, and allow love, or something larger than yourself, to guide you. Cleanse yourself and your lover from the cares of the day with a bath, a fresh dose of perfume, or a mental housecleaning. Gather all the materials you'll need, take some deep breaths, and invite a mood of mystery, romance, and divine delirium to enter your soul.

Ingredient #2: Atmosphere.

Romantic, mystical, or simply *changed* surroundings break the spell of the everday and transport you to a sensation-rich realm where only the two of you exist. Make your room into a bacchanalian den of love with lots of candles, a favorite incense you use only for ritual, fur or satin bed coverings, erotic pictures, scented love oils, dimmed or colored lighting, and flowers – perhaps red hibiscus, with their boldly protruding stamens and passionate crimson color. Or create a Zen-like sanctuary with everything in creamy whites and beiges, newly crisp or linen sheets, and just one exquisite calla (arum) lily or sculpture. You may want to design a love altar with icons special to the two of you or consecrate a floor blanket to act as your playpen. Put on a diaphanous robe, veils and jangly jewelry, or nothing but a pearl necklace, dressing the part of the goddess or siren you aim to invoke. The idea is for both of you to walk in and think, 'Wow! I've entered another world. Let's make some sex magic!'

Ingredient #3: Significant Acts.

Out-of-the-ordinary events are the heart and soul of ritual. Mark the beginning of your ceremony by offering a gift to each other, ringing a melodic bell, anointing each other with sweet oil, or simply inviting the spirit of passion, fun, or love to join you. Exchange long, pregnant gazes and praise each other with ethereal names and loving compliments. Use the massage, bathing, or intense petting in your ritual to prolong foreplay to fever pitch. Then let your glorified sensations and otherworldly imagination spill over into exalted lovemaking. Close by reverently disassembling your temporary sanctuary, sharing some refreshments, or simply blowing out the candles.

Instant Ritual

It doesn't *have* to be elaborate or time-consuming. You can ritualize, and therefore elevate, even a white-hot quickie. Just use the barest hint of each of the three elements described above, concentrating heavily on the mental preparation. For example, you might vividly fantasize about the divinity of your body and your partner; light some incense, take him outside for the rarefied atmosphere, or don one piece of clothing that makes you look and feel divine; then worship and set aflame what you have now transmuted into his mighty Sword of Shiva. It's the intention that counts.

ritual baths

258. *Champagne Bath.* Soap bubbles are fun, but champagne (and the pouring of it) elevates bathing to a whole other level. Gather some inexpensive bubbly, two crystal goblets, scented soap, and a small plastic bowl. Put on your slave girl mentality along with a brief little bath toga, and create atmosphere with candles, piles of fluffy towels, and perhaps statuettes of nude goddesses. Standing naked in the hot water with your man, pour champagne between your cleaved-together bodies, letting it cascade off your thighs into the bath. Take a sip and spurt the bubbly liquid over his chest, back, and genitals. Kiss him with champagne flowing from your mouth.

Then give him a goblet of elixir and ask him to sit. Raise one of his arms or legs and set it on yours, tenderly washing it with a loofah. Rinse by dipping your plastic bowl in the bathwater and pouring slowly from it, as if anointing him. When you're done washing each body part, cradle him with your body from behind and caress his chest and thighs or pour hot water over his head and neck. Finish by reverently toweling him dry and sending him out the door with a kiss.

259. *Foot Washing.* An ancient sign of respect and fealty to a king, this will make your man feel royally pampered. Prepare a deep bowl with hot water, collect scented oil and towels, and set him up in a comfy chair. Incense, music, and soft lighting complete the atmosphere. Kiss each foot as you lovingly place it in the water; then serve him a drink, read to him, or massage his hands while he soaks. After a few minutes, attentively wash his softened feet. Alternatively, rinse his feet with a fluffy cloth dipped in the pure water and then both of you take a sip from the bowl, creating an immediate and especially deep ceremonial bond. Either way, follow up with a scented-oil foot massage, making sure to sensually rub his arches and the cleavage between all toes. End by reverently kissing your king's feet once again.

260. *Shampooing.* Prepare by imagining yourself a sensual masseuse in an ancient temple of love. Invite your man into the candlelit bathroom for a de-stressing scalp massage, and arrange him in a chair with his head arching

comfortably backward into the sink, neck supported on a rolled towel. Hand him a goblet of wine, light some lavender incense (because it's calming and one of men's favorite scents), and perhaps lay a warm towel over his eyes. Use a spray attachment or pitcher to thoroughly wet his hair, and then apply scented or tingly shampoo to your hand before weaving it through his hair. Massage his scalp, temples, and hairline in small circles and squeeze the foam from the roots of the hair to the ends, allowing your perfumed breast to hover near his face. Rinse, and apply a fruity conditioner, kissing his eyelids and brow while it soaks in. Finally, pour to rinse and wrap his head in a thick, warm towel. Blow out the candles and bow out.

ceremonial spaces

261. *Design a sex altar.* An altar provides a focus for your sensual intention and creates a little energy vortex that attracts the spirits of love and romance. Every time you pass by, it will trigger your feelings of womanly eroticism. And if you invite your man to participate in putting together the altar, it will encourage him to view sex as magic, rather than as a goal or a performance.

Cover a small chest or table with a beautiful red or purple cloth and place upon it several things that remind you of the depth of your sexual feelings – red candles, jasmine incense, perhaps a phallic stone and a vagina-like shell, a statue of Aphrodite and/or Adonis, a photo of you and your lover, a memento from a romantic vacation, a love note, a favorite sex toy. Beginning any sensual ritual by lighting the candles and incense or simply touching the icons on your altar will add pageantry and a sense of the numinous. And simply having it in the room will flavor your everyday lovemaking with the sublime.

262. *Enshrine your bed.* Consecrated places create the stage for holy events. My altarlike bed is draped overhead with sheer Balinese silk in the summer and velvet, fox fur, and ceremonial feathers in the winter. You might hang an elegant lace chemise or an embroidered kimono from the bedpost and place dramatic candlesticks on each nightstand. Dress the bed in a downy quilt and stack a bazillion velvety, satin, or Egyptian cotton pillows at its head. Furry rugs beside the bed invite kneeling and provide a cushion for positions that require leverage. The ancient Romans often bedecked their sleeping couches with a figure of the patron god or goddess of their particular marriage. Some icon of your love – a special photo; a stuffed lion because you're both Leos; the veil, prayer shawl, or ribbons from your wedding or trousseau – should be the final sacred touch.

263. *Romantic* Feng Shui. According to this ancient Chinese art, where you position furniture and knick-knacks can either

deaden or enliven crucial parts of your life. To ensure that vitality, freshness, and inspiration are always flowing in your romantic life, feng shui the Love and Marriage corner of your home, bedroom, and sexual altar. As you enter your house or room (or face the altar), this area lies in the right rear corner. Remove any clutter there and embellish the space with pairs of things (flowers, hearts, doves, symbols of love); pictures of you and your real-life or ideal lover; items in red, pink, and white; quotes about love and sensuality; love goddesses; live plants; wind chimes; beautiful lamps or candles; honeymoon mementos; mirrors; water features; and personal icons of romance.

My Love and Marriage corners include six-foot-tall plants, statues of couples in loving embrace, African sexual amulets, and pairs of exotic candlesticks. Even the right rear corner of my desk is adorned with a photo of my beloved – the man who came into my life shortly after I feng shuied my entire apartment. And every time I add fresh flowers or symbolic items to one of these areas, our relationship and our bedplay take off in juicy new directions.

sensual massage rituals

Sensual massage is one of the most prized erotic arts of the Orient. Aside from soothing and relaxing, deep skin contact actually releases a tantalizing brew of hormones and adds another few rungs to the ladder of orgasmic pleasure. Any massage can be elevated to a rite of Eros if you include candlelight, scented massage oil, ethereal or sultry music, ultrasoft sheets, and the intention to summon the sylphs of love.

264. *Naked Therapy.* Invite your man into a very warm and ritually appointed room where you are his nude Aphroditic masseuse. Lie him facedown and begin by barely stroking his entire body with fingers filled with erotic electricity. Straddle his hips so he can feel the warmth of your inner thighs, and apply almond-scented oil to your hands, perhaps drizzling it down his back as well. As you knead and squeeze, allow your hair and nipples to graze his skin, leaning forward to press against him and lick or blow on his ear. When you dismount, run your oiled hands up his inner thighs and around his buttocks before asking him to turn over.

If he is on the floor, kneel at his head and graze his face and chest with your tresses, breasts, and pubic hair as you stroke the front of his body. Working from the outer extremities, finally arrive at the hub of his manhood, first polishing his perineum in firm circles. Then remount and deepen your massaging, body presses, and nibbles; or sit between his legs to delight him with some of the manual phallus-worship techniques from chapter 6. End with woman-on-top love-making or cover him with a cozy blanket and let him drift off to erotic dreamland.

265. ***Acupressure aphrodisia.*** By concentrating on certain hot spots, you can open the doors to his hidden erotic nature. Using the ancient tradition of anointing (which conferred royalty upon a king or awoke latent psychic powers), daub a tiny bit of oil on his eyelids, the valley between his brows, and any other pleasure point you wish to impassion, praising each part as you touch it. Then palpate, lick, tap, flick, or press your pointed breasts against any or all of these especially electric 'inlets':

- tips of toes and fingers
- around, not on, knees
- hollows of hipbone and clavicle
- two inches below navel
- top of cheekbone
- inside of elbow
- secret erection center in back (see page 118)
- earlobes
- underside of wrist
- next to spine at waist
- between shoulder blades
- sweet spot of buttocks
- head of penis
- top edge of pubic hairline

266. ***Man-Handling.*** Pour him a drink, turn on some Miles Davis and low lights, and worship the hands that work so hard to support and please you. First soak them in a bowl of warm water with hair conditioner in it. Then, one hand at a time, pull with long strokes from his wrist to his fingertips. Circle your thumbs in his palms and knead each finger between your thumb and first two fingers. Gazing into his eyes, kiss his palm and suck each finger as if it were a small penis. Finish by enclosing his hand lovingly between both of yours as you tell him how sensual and alive his hands make you feel. Or place his now-tingling fingers gently on your breast and let him take it from there.

intimate ceremonies

267. *Shaving Ritual (for him).* A titillating way to build deep trust and intimacy, the venerable art of shaving pubic hair has been around for centuries. While your man may be reluctant at first, you can: (1) explain that it will greatly increase his genital sensitivity; (2) say you can't wait to shower lots of kisses on his bare pubis; (3) promise to let him shave you.

Gather small scissors, a razor that's been used only once or twice, a shaving brush and cream, a basin of warm water, a flannel, and baby oil. Clad in filmy lingerie, make an elegant entrance with your tools and a vase of flowers on a tray. Prop him up with pillows and tell him how manly and gorgeous his Lance of Love is as you carefully trim the surrounding hair with scissors. Then apply a hot wet flannel to the short fuzz, softening it for easier removal. Finally, smooth on the shaving cream and *carefully* render him hairless. Rub on soothing baby oil (or witch hazel) to prevent razor burn as you coo over his freshly exposed virility. For a stirring conclusion, decorate him with garlands, wide ribbon, or scarves; groom and tickle his weapon with the clean shaving brush; and/or massage the oiled, babylike skin of his entire genital area.

268. *Shaving ritual (for you).* Present him with a hand-lettered invitation to your virgin shaving ritual. Designate a time and place and provide instructions that include his being naked (he'll feel more vulnerable that way and will take greater care with the delicate operation). Assemble all the materials for him (with the addition of a camera) and make the atmosphere as comfortable, safe, and resplendent as you desire. You may want to bathe first to make your hair soft and easy to remove. At the end of the ceremony, ask him to take a photo of your bare beauty that he can keep tucked away very deeply in his wallet.

Penis-Pleasuring Ceremony

Like an ancient love priestess, you can take your man to nirvana by approaching his Magic Wand with the devotion and worship it deserves. After all, it does provide both of you with the most exquisite rapture.

- Prepare the room with flowers, candles, scented oils, and a bowl of pure water, as was done for ancient rites of phallus worship. Now is a good time to make use of your sexual altar, perhaps centering a phallic icon on it.

- Enthrone your king on velvety or satin cushions, so he's half-reclining, comfortable, and well-exposed.

- Approach him with reverence and playful devotion, naked except for a single flower in your hair. Wear red lipstick so the visual of lips on genitals is vividly accentuated. Do everything slowly and ritually.

- Kneel at his feet and bathe his sacred organ with a soft, hot flannel.

- Cradle it lovingly in your hand and say something like, 'I have come to worship this delicious Scepter of Love that makes me feel like a goddess.'

- If you are going to adore him manually, anoint the head of his penis, testicles, and perineum with scented oil. Then overlubricate your hands and rub them all over his entire genital area and belly. Milk his love organ gently until it's swollen with desire, and then perform your favorite techniques from 'The Handmaid's Tradition' section of chapter 6, page 92.

- If you will be idolizing him orally, focus all your erotic feelings inside your mouth and begin by licking and stroking his inner thighs and belly. Treating his member like a delicate flower, lick softly on the head until he stiffens. Use some old reliable and some exotic untried techniques from 'The Oral Tradition' section of chapter 6, page 80, occasionally pausing to lick your lips and say 'Mmmm.'
- Keep up whatever he has liked best until his juices flow. Lap them up like honey or collect the sacred nectars and smear them rapturously over your breasts and pubis.
- Let him slowly descend from the Himalayas while you lightly caress his thighs, stomach, and buttocks, still holding him warmly in your mouth or hands.
- When you're ready, slowly release him, wash him reverently with the warm cloth, and cover his body with a soft blanket. Either cuddle him to sleep or bow out of his presence elegantly.

11

hot tantra and other secrets from the orient

Come into my sensual reclining form . . . Make your throbbing diamond-hard weapon of love enter into the heart of my silky soft Lotus! Give thousands of loving strokes to my fleshy three-petaled Lotus love-flower. Insert your precious Vajra and sacrifice your mind with pleasure!

—*Chandamaharosana Tantra*

The ancient Indians and Chinese (as well as the Polynesians and Native Americans) believed that sex was a sacred gift from the gods, and that women were the key to unwrapping it. In fact, men were taught to please a woman to the peaks of multiorgasmic ecstasy – a divine state that she could in turn bestow upon her lover.

To achieve that level of smolder, the ancient sages advised men to slow down and 'give worship [to women] in one's soul even as to one's guru.' Women were advised to simply enjoy by tuning deeply into their bodies and sensations. For example, when he is 'worshiping' you with very deep penetration, focus your attention on the exact spot where his thrusting organ is buried. By drinking in each luscious impact, you will feel a more intense rapture there – a well of sensation that rises up to saturate every cell in your potent, female body. Glowing with an aura of sex, you are a woman capable of transforming an ordinary roll in the hay into the electric coupling of the gods.

Tantric Sizzle

While in their purest form the sexual practices of Tantra and the Tao may seem too foreign or complicated for us, we Westerners can adapt some of their techniques to add just as much Oriental kindling to our love fire as we want.

- **Smolder.** In Oriental lovemaking, there are many postures in which movement is severely limited. But if you assume these positions only *after* you've come to a passionate boil (say, a delicious hour of foreplay and teasing penetration), then you can remain in a simmering preclimactic state for a long, agonizingly ecstatic time.
- **Electrify your senses.** The Tantricas and Taoists deliberately cultivated a heightened awareness of each physical sensation. Like them, revel in the feel of skin sliding against skin; the sound of ragged breathing and slapping thighs; the scent of his potent pheromones; the ripe look of a flushed nipple; the pulsing of your lover's heartbeat; and the delicious swelling of your own vulva. These intensified sensations ricochet, like heated laser beams, within and between you.
- **Imagine yourselves as deities of love.** Part of the power and fun of Eastern lovemaking is worshiping each other as god and goddess. Elevate yourself to the stature of Aphrodite; or the sinuous Minoan Snake Goddess; or the Native American Fire Woman, who initiates young men into the ways of pleasing. Lavishly praise your lover's Adonis-like form, his brawny Atlas muscles, the magnificence of his Sword of Eros. Take on the roles of Shiva and Shakti birthing the universe through their divine lovemaking,

or the Dark Girl mentoring the Yellow Emperor in mutual sexual inquiry. All these exalted personages, embodied in you, make inspired, divine love.

- **Trigger your passion with words.** The beautiful Oriental terms for the genitals are enough to induce a state of rapture all by themselves. For you: Precious Gateway, Flower Heart, Pleasure Field of Heaven, Honey Pot, Enchanted Garden, Golden Crevice, Cinnabar Grotto. For him: Rainbow Serpent, Healing Scepter, Jade Stalk, Wand of Light, Celestial Dragon, Mushroom of Immortality, Crimson Bird. Use these names in your lovemaking and invite their evocative images to set your mind, heart, and libido afire.
- **Concentrate on the 'Sizzle'.** The complex, gravity-defying postures of the Orient always have a purpose – for example, deep penetration, good sight lines, maximum female pleasure. So to get the most out of any position, skip the intricate toe placement and zoom in mentally on the specified 'Sizzle.' Much like the way a vivid fantasy actually heats your blood and tingles your skin, your focused attention will turn up the flames on that sensation, searing it even more deeply into your body – and into his.

the steamy openers

269. ***The Heavenly Hug.*** Lovely as a prelude to lovemaking or a bonding technique with which to start your day, this sweet embrace can either calm or stir the blood, depending on your intention. Kneel, facing each other, then sit back on your feet and scoot forward till your knees touch his. Lean forward, placing your head (turned to the side) deeply into his lap, and rest your hands on his thighs. He enwraps you by leaning forward to lay the side of his face on the middle of your back, hands on your lower back. Breathe slowly together and melt even more deeply into the embrace. Switch positions whenever you feel ready. The Sizzle: hot breath on genitals, skin-to-skin sparks, deep soul-stirring communion.

270. ***The Kama Sutra Kiss.*** Tantricas kiss not only to enjoy the lush sensuality of it, but also to mix their love nectars and build intensity. So, whether during foreplay or entangled in some puzzlelike posture, take the time to make a sensory art of it. Run the tip of your rough tongue languidly across his satiny lips; plant scores of tiny tender kisses and contrasting nibbles along his lower lip; use your tongue to thrust like a penis and your lips to squeeze like a vagina; and finally invite his piercing tongue into the yielding softness of your mouth (symbolic of that other hard-into-

soft penetration), drinking in the rich elixir of each other's hot saliva. The Sizzle: extenuated, dizzying lip sensations, reminiscent of when you made out for hours as teens; the heat and electric tingle of each other's breath.

271. *The Nibbling of the Wild Boar.* According to the *Kama Sutra,* biting is one of the best ways to awaken sleeping passions. As you and your lover begin to pant with desire, you may wish to administer a few discreet but attention-getting lip crunches to his neck, ears, nipples, or inner thighs. Whether you seize a small piece of skin between your teeth and pull, or simply rake your fangs across sensitized flesh, the Tantric love manual promises that 'love will never decrease, even after one hundred years.' The Sizzle: surprise, contrast, intense sensation, the unabashed expression of animal lust.

272. *The Chinese Plum.* Make a little cap for your man's penis by opening one side of a firm plum and removing the pit. Set it atop his upright sex and squeeze it slightly so juice trickles down the shaft. When the time is ripe, he thrusts his hooded weapon deeply inside you. At some point, the little fruit will come off in your vagina, and you can challenge him to retrieve it with his tongue. Once it's recaptured, you can either smoosh it all over each other's hot skin or eat it. The Sizzle: exotic, fruity taste; extra fullness and squishiness inside you.

273. *The Sacred 69.* In Eastern love-making, the blending of oral and genital love juices is thought to produce a healing elixir for both partners. All of these benefits are enhanced if your mutual genital kiss is performed in a slightly elevated position. Have him sit on the floor with legs straight out in front and hands slightly behind him. He should raise himself slightly off the floor, using a pillow if necessary. You stand about six inches beyond his head, facing his feet, and lean forward to support yourself with hands on the floor beside his thighs. This should put your mouth and Precious Pearl in the proper positions for reciprocal licking. If you are really flexible, you can turn around and do a back bend atop your lucky man, arching your neck back to play his Magic Flute while offering the ripe peaches of your behind and vulva to his eager lips. The Sizzle: increased swelling and tingling sensations in the loins; the sheer thrill of adventure.

missionary positions from heaven

274. *Foot Fetish.* Tantricas believe that the feet are filled with high-voltage sex energy (hence the tickle factor) and often incorporate them into standard coitus to make it hotter. In the missionary position, fold your knees to your chest so he can grasp your feet to use them as little springboards for his thrusting. The Sizzle: *deep*

penetration, G-spot heaven, the feel of his masterful control, added sensation in soles of feet.

275. *Phoenix Plays in a Red Cave.* Lying on your back, grasp your feet and raise them high in the air, providing a beautifully flagrant invitation for him to enter. The Sizzle: spread-wide-open feeling; his pelvis rubbing against your bottom.

276. *Foot-to-Heart Connection.* You can intensify his feelings of love when, lying in the missionary position, you bring your thighs together and place your sexually charged feet on his chest. The Sizzle: tightened and sensitized vagina lips; feel of his chest hair and/or waves of ardor on the soles of your feet.

277. *Giant Bird Soaring over a Dark Sea.* Lying on your back, raise your knees and curl your bent legs around his elbows so your calves are outside his arms. Clasp your hands around his neck. The Sizzle: deep penetration; feeling of delicious exposure and soaring; arouses lusty passion.

278. *Crouching Tiger.* From the missionary posture, make an 'L' with your legs by holding the left one straight up and sliding the right one out at a right angle to your body. Grasp your right knee with your right arm. He squats with his left foot planted in the triangle made by

your right leg and arm, while your left leg lies against his chest. You may want to boost your pelvis with a pillow. The Sizzle: unrestrained, very deep thrusting; stimulation of rarely reached spots in the vagina.

279. *Swimming Turtle.* Lie on your back and plant your feet on the bed, close to your bottom. With your hands on the bed, helping to support you, freely raise, circle, and undulate your pelvic 'turtle' in any direction you please. The Sizzle: unexcelled freedom of movement; control of timing, positioning, and impact.

280. *Love Bloom.* Don't overlook this subtle but extremely powerful technique. During standard missionary sex, focus on the throbbing, hot energy in your vulva and mentally raise it up to your heart. Concentrate intently on the feel of ecstasy and orgasmic bliss in this new location. The Sizzle: As my friend Deborah says. 'It adds a whole other feeling, one of connectedness'; also great for building desire when your mind is willing and able but your body isn't.

side by side

281. *Heavenly Scissors.* Recline on your side and open your legs like a scissors. On his knees, he straddles your lower leg and inserts his weapon. You can control the depth of his thrusting

and your juicy tightness by raising and lowering your upper leg and/or lifting your entire pelvis. The Sizzle: intriguing angles of penetration; pressure and stimulation on your perineum and bottom.

282. *Spoon Rest.* In the basic spoon position, thrust and parry until near orgasm. Then stop, focus on breathing together, and imagine hot energy flowing between your nestled genitals, chest areas, and heads. Resume thrusting, and then pause again near climax. The Sizzle: palpable and intimate electric charge between you, the feel of his hot breath on your neck, heart pounding against your back, genitals throbbing all around yours.

bliss from behind

283. *Prone Paradise.* Lie facedown with legs together, and invite him to kneel astride your bottom and enter you from behind. You can either reach back to clasp his forearms for leverage, or ask him to pummel and rub your back. The Sizzle: pressure of clitoris sliding against bed; snug fit where you can feel *everything.*

284. *Cleaving the Cicada.* Again, you lie facedown on the bed, but this time his thighs are *inside* yours and he is actually lying on your back. He should 'cleave your cicada' by reaching

underneath to lift, open, and caress your labial lips while rocking and thrusting his Scepter inside you. The Sizzle: feeling of being 'taken'; and, according to Felice Dunas in her fabulous book *Passion Play,* you become so aroused that your vulva throbs and spreads open.

285. *Donkeys of Late Spring.* Get on your hands and feet, with your knees slightly bent and your inviting bottom as high in the air as possible. Let your head hang down so you can peek between your legs as he inserts his Wand of Light from a standing position. The Sizzle: great new views; heightened vaginal sensation and extraordinary G-spot stimulation; the feel of his free-standing, ravaging thrusts.

stand and worship

286. *Splitting Bamboo.* Limber up beforehand by stretching your legs high on a ballet bar and doing lunges. Then the next time you are standing face-to-face kissing, you can fulfill the male fantasy of having sex with a gymnast. Raise one of your legs, first to dangle your knee over his bent elbow, and then to extend a straight leg over his shoulder. He can assist by clasping his hands behind your back, his arms circling around the outside of your leg. The Sizzle: a piercing angle of penetration; oscillating and fierce clitoral contact.

287. ***Tantric Wheelbarrow.*** Get on your elbows and knees, and lower the side of your face to the floor. Invite him to walk up to you from the rear and lift your ankles to either side of his waist so he can hold you as he would a wheelbarrow. Reveling in the feeling of power and high kink, he can gently rock you to and fro on his Jade Stalk while you enjoy the ride. The Sizzle: upside-down blood-rushes to never-before-awakened spots; G-spot invigoration.

288. ***Suspended Congress.*** The famous and evocative pose seen in many Tantric sculptures – wherein the man stands while his lover literally hangs from him with her arms clasped around his neck, legs wrapped around his waist, and his hands holding her up by the bottom – can be accomplished by regular humans if one of you leans your back against a wall for support. If he is the one so bolstered, you can brace your feet against the wall and push yourself back and forth over his Wand of Light. In the reverse situation, he can suspend you on the wall and, feeling like a mighty Hercules, pound into you vigorously. Better yet, use the buoyancy afforded when you stand in water to keep you elevated. The Sizzle: thrilling suspension and sense of danger; fiery genital energy shooting straight up your spine.

goddess on top

289. *Kali's Pose.* Have him lie faceup, with his legs slightly bent and feet on the bed. You mount him, on your knees, and sit regally erect, arching your back just enough to reach behind and rest your hands on his knees. Squeeze his shaft with your powerful inner rings, and use your thigh muscles to raise and lower your whole torso over his lap. The Sizzle: distended breasts and clitoral tissue bared for his touch; the sensation of his Healing Scepter buried deep within you in an acutely angled position; the thrill of queenly control.

290. *King for a Night.* Prepare his royal seat by stacking pillows near the edge of the bed and have him sit there with his legs hanging over. You then mount him, your knees on either side of his hips, your hands resting on his pillowy throne, and your breasts perfectly placed to receive his kingly kiss. The Sizzle: comfort; the delicious control of angle and depth; simultaneous G-spot and nipple stimulation.

291. *King for a Night II.* This time his throne is a soft chair. You sit atop his Royal Scepter, then lean back just enough to maneuver each of your feet up to his shoulders and straighten your legs. Slide to and fro in his lap, or place your fists beside his hips and, with straight

arms, leverage yourself up and down. Thrusting atop him, your Golden Doorway is majestically presented for his view and caress. The Sizzle: premier G-spot and clitoral stimulation; relishing the ecstatic smile on his face.

292. *The Snake.* Anoint your bodies with oil, then lie atop him, both of you stretched out straight. With his Celestial Dragon inside you, press, glide, and slither your whole body back and forth over his. You can also squeeze your legs together and rub, circle your hips, and/or slide your oiled nipples across his chest. He will love the new and provocative sensation of your full weight pressing and sliding against him. The Sizzle: tactile and slippery stimulation of entire body; the feel of pinning him.

293. *Lady Wang's Delight.* He lies prone; you straddle his hips on your knees, facing his feet. There are several delicious things you can do from here: lean forward to brace your hands on the bed and then rock back and forth on his severely angled Jade Emperor; massage his feet and lick his toes; sit up straight and caress both your genitals between your legs; arch back and rest your hands on his chest, then grind and bounce your hips seductively. While the Ripe Peaches of your behind graze against his pelvis and belly (Lady Wang is the keeper of the peaches of immortality), he can stroke and ogle your bottom and beautifully arched back. The Sizzle:

unequaled control of new angles of penetration; great G-spot contact; soft scratches and caresses on back and bottom.

294. *Shakti in Spring.* With him lying on his back and you seated atop his Pleasure Limb (facing his feet), bring your feet between his legs and up close to his jewels. Support yourself by placing your hands on his thighs and spring up and down. You can also move both your feet outside one of his hips, just to get a new perspective on things and vary your queenly bounce. The Sizzle: fabulous control and agility; the feel of his hands, free to caress you almost everywhere; omnidirectional views.

295. *The Cobra Uncoiled.* Have him lie prone while you kneel astride his pelvis, facing forward. Lean way back, grasping his ankles for support (perhaps bending his knees to bring his feet closer to you). If you are flexible enough, you can extend this graceful stretch by arching your head down and back to touch the bed. Reveling in the view of your elongated curves, he will not be able to resist fondling your beautifully exposed Rosebud of Delight. The Sizzle: the feel of being stretched open wide in passionate abandon; super stimulation to the G-spot and deep inner recesses.

296. *Lions in Repose.* Sit astride his hips, facing forward, as he lies on his back. Place your feet next to his shoulders and lower your

torso to the bed between his legs, forming an 'X' with your two bodies. You can both clasp hands and counterbalance each other's thrusts, or you can simply lie there like a languid lion, wriggling your hips and using plenty of Kegel clenches to keep him purring. The Sizzle: lovely relaxation and a disembodied floaty feeling; the freedom to concentrate on your inner pulses; the gripping embrace of your hands.

297. *Flying Dragons.* Try to briefly incorporate this wild posture into your lovemaking, just for the luscious insanity of it all. Starting from a bent-kneed prone position, he pushes himself up with his hands next to his chest, his calves and straight arms perpendicular to the rest of his body. His torso forms a plank. You then hop astride and lean forward to touch your breasts to his chest. Here's where the delightful madness reaches its peak: Supporting yourself with your right hand and foot on the floor, lift your left ankle, grasp it with your left hand, and bring it close to your bottom. He can toss his pelvis up and down while you fly your left 'wing' to and fro atop him. The Sizzle: If you don't collapse on the floor in gales of laughter (a superior aphrodisiac), you can both permanently activate your Superman chakras just by being able to achieve this pose one time.

the classic yum yum

The position where the man sits cross-legged on the floor and you sit in his lap with your legs locked behind his back, arms entwined around his neck, is called the Yab Yum. In this most classic of all Tantric positions, you are literally locked together in love. Considered the sacred posture of the gods, the purpose of this position is to lend wings to the loving energy in both yours and your lover's genitals, so it can rise up through your hearts, into your lips and eyes, and travel across to your mate, circulating around again in a continuous oval of adoration. That's why I prefer to call it the Yum Yum.

Making the Yum Yum Even Yummier

Yum Yum Sizzle: Though it doesn't allow for real thrusting, the Yum Yum results in very deep penetration, high-level G-spot stimulation, direct clitoral touch, and intense face-to-face, heart-to-heart intimacy. It can make a woman feel as if her whole body is a vulva, with his Scepter of Light glowing all the way up to her forehead; and a man may sense that her Valley of Joy has completely engulfed him, turning his entire body into throbbing, pulsing male essence.

Yum Yum hint: He can sit on a firm pillow

to lessen the extreme stretch of his legs. Or, to take some of the weight off his thighs, you can sit on a pillow yourself.

Yummy activities: While languidly locked in the classic Yum Yum posture, you can: (1) gaze deeply into each other's eyes and whisper uplifting compliments and words of adoration; (2) kiss passionately, feeding on each other's mouth nectars; (3) gently rock and sway your hips in rapturous rhythm; (4) allow your hands to roam caressingly over each other's faces, breasts, backs, limbs, and pelvic mounds; (5) hypnotically milk his shaft and heighten your arousal by pulsing your PCs; (6) raise and lower a knee to vary angles and sensations; (7) sit locked together lip-to-lip, nipple-to-nipple, belly-to-belly, genitals fused, and breathe deeply of each other's perfume (lusciously loving as a pre- or postcoital transition).

298. ***Non-yab Yum.*** Sit in the classic posture, but with his Jade Stalk jutting upright between you instead of resting in your Moist Cave. Look liquidly into his eyes as you stroke, press, and knead his throbbing limb.

299. ***Deep Yum Yum.*** Drape your legs over his elbows, burying him even further inside you. Undulate sensuously. As an added aesthetic, point your toes to make an elegant curved line with your legs.

300. *Yum Yum Massage.* Lean back slightly so you can easily reach his feet. Lovingly massage his toes, soles, and insteps, slowly sliding one finger between each of his toes in imitation of his usual thrusts inside you.

301. *Yum Yum Tango.* Unwrap your legs and brace them on the floor behind his back. If you support yourself further by placing your hands on the floor behind you, your hips are free to dance, grind, and circle sinuously, driving him wild with near-to-orgasm pulsations.

302. *Tantric Love Grip.* In the Yum Yum position, clasp each other's forearms and both lean back as far as you can, throwing your heads back so that the fronts of your bodies are stretched open. Focus on your Flower Heart, pulsing and encircling his Magic Wand in a grip of love. Then let your hands slide from forearms to wrists and lean back even further, lowering the tops of your heads to the floor if possible. In this new grip of trusting abandon, pull each other upright and fall back repeatedly, until the resulting inner friction has ignited an orgasmic fire. The Sizzle: the extended line of your torso, from genitals to throat, sensitized by the exaggerated stretch; euphoria induced by blood rushing to your head; the feeling of throw-your-head-back abandon; the extenuated, intense buildup of genital heat.

The Love Coronation

- Set aside a special time and place, worthy of sacred activities. Tantricas consider the hours between midnight and three a.m. especially potent, but any quiet time will do. Prepare the space with candles, flowers, incense, sacred love objects, food and wine. These intoxicating items are meant to attract the gods and goddesses of love to your sanctuary and elevate your thoughts and feelings.
- Ritually bathe each other to cleanse away the day's cares and purify you for the highest loving.
- Adorn yourself in queenly style – perhaps something red, something translucent, or just one piece of dramatic jewelry.
- Anoint your king. Apply scented oil to his feet, pubic mound, nipples and heart area, throat, and forehead, with the intention of awakening his most divine attributes. Ask him to anoint you in similar fashion.
- Light the candles and drink a toast – first to the fire of passion; then to the God of Love, who sits before you, embodied in your lover; and finally to yourself as the Divine Goddess and sensual Initiatrix of Enlightenment.

- Begin caressing your beloved, your hands pouring adoration into his skin. Plant sweet kisses all over his body, finally arriving at his Golden Scepter. Lick him to throbbing arousal, but no further.
- Offer your Pleasure Field of Heaven to his lips just long enough to bring the Goddess of Passion into your own loins. Perhaps indulge in some mutual oral delights.
- Move into divine congress any way you like. One suggestion is to first take your pleasure atop him, like the queen you are. From there it's easy to sit up into the Yum Yum position, kissing deeply, breathing each other's hot breath, and feeling currents of love course through your entire body. Then lay back into some version of the missionary position, praising his might and kingliness, and keeping him on the verge by applying the squeeze technique as necessary. Perhaps pause to refresh yourselves with strawberries, wine, and hot words of love, and then resume your divine union in a side-by-side or rear-entry position, pleasuring each other's pubic areas by hand simultaneously. Bring each other near to climax several times, surrendering to the irresistible impulses building within, before finally dissolving in the bliss of a cosmic orgasm.

- Lie in each other's arms and whisper words of praise and devotion.
- When the time is right, bring an elegant close to the ritual by thanking him for bringing out the goddess in you and letting you see the god in him. Then reverently disassemble your love sanctuary until the next time.

12

training your man

Half the time, if you really want to know the truth, when I'm horsing around and with a girl, I have a helluva lot of trouble just finding what I'm looking for, for God's sake, if you know what I mean.

—J. D. Salinger,
The Catcher in the Rye

I once had a lover who, though skilled in the sexual ABCs, didn't know how to find what both of us were really looking for. He thought he wanted more orgasms. I knew I wanted more passionate, soul-stirring lovemaking. Since he wasn't getting us there, I decided to take the lead.

Thinking I was going to change *him,* I consciously practiced the time-honored arts of seduction. As I walked with a wiggle and thought about sex more often, I noticed that my body became more fluid and my senses woke up to recognize a million shades of blue and the many subtle textures of my lover's beard. I found myself crossing new sexual frontiers and feeling like a sassy but classy strumpet. In bed, my hands took on a life of their own, finding new ways to caress, tease, and burnish his skin. My rediscovered sensuality, radiating at solar wattage, seemed to pierce his unconscious armor and awaken some magic within him. Gradually he began to make love to me more sensitively yet powerfully, to worship as well as ravish my body. Together we became virtuosic lovers.

I had come to understand that men, who are built to strive for and attain goals, usually don't know how to enjoy the journey. Especially when it comes to sex, their bodies and minds become even more firm and single-pointed. We women, on the other hand, open up in the act of making love, inviting penetration, emotion, and revelation to course through our flesh and hearts.

It's up to us, then, as keepers of the mysteries of

love, to initiate our men into the secrets of their own sensuality, and to train them in the arts of romance, foreplay, and deeply erotic lovemaking. We need to encourage them to be explorers rather than armored warriors; to brandish a Magic Wand instead of a Big Showy Sword. We need to wield the power we have always had, but seldom used, to mold our men into the lovers of our dreams.

gaining his ear

Often the first challenge is getting him to listen. How do you make him receptive to the pearls of your wisdom? How do you open his heart?

- **Praise him.** While women ache to feel beautiful and sexy, men need to feel heroic and effective. So even before it becomes true, praise him for being powerful, kingly, and brave, for being a master at providing everything you desire. Tell him often how much his manliness turns you on. Magically, he will soon start to believe and live up to your image of him.
- **Learn his language.** Women like to talk; but men respond to touch. With them, a sensual caress speaks louder than a thousand words. Squeeze his arm as you pass by, casually fondle his member while you watch TV, graze his cheek with your fingers before telling him something important. You will sensitize his skin, soften his heart, and open his ears.

- **Inspire him.** Instead of wanting him to be someone he isn't, inspire him to be more of who he is. Believe in him. Envision greatness for him. Be so womanly, so beautiful, so soft, so sensitive and wise that you set aflame his desire to be man enough to win you. Trigger his imagination and he will discover original ways to please you.
- **Flatter him by revealing details about himself.** Most men don't have a clue what their most compelling assets are. Tell him how his long eyelashes and smoky blue eyes are the envy of all your friends, or that the little hollow under his left collarbone is outrageously sexy. Divulge to him that, 'No one has ever tickled my navel the way you do, with that sexy little flip of your tongue.' He will feel unique, cherished, and eager to know more.
- **Start where it counts.** For women, love opens the door to sex. For men, sex is the doorway to love. His erotic feelings, many of his emotions, and often his ability to reason are centered in his phallus. Begin there – with compliments, touch, and yearning gazes – and you can go almost anywhere.

getting him to do what you like in bed

- **Tell him.** Men are basically mystified, so simple instructions are appreciated. At the same time, though, they recoil from too much direction. So couch your suggestions in sincere flattery, love, and even humor. You might say, 'Mmmm, I love that. And it's even more sensitive a little to the right . . . Oh, yesssss!' Or 'I adore having you inside, but let's wait until I can't bear it anymore.'

- **Act as if he's already done it.** Rave about how good it was, how much it turned you on, how you can't wait for more. Glow with satisfaction.
- **Move his hands.** Place them exactly where you'd like them to be, even interlocking your fingers with his to assist in getting the right pressure, speed, and direction. Then moan to let him know how fantastic it feels.
- **Move your body.** Be bold. If you want him to pay more attention to your breasts, graze your nipple across his lips. If you crave deeper G-spot stimulation, flip yourself over and offer him the tantalizing rear entry that provides it. Reinforce his responses with sighs and screams of delight.
- **Read him 'customized' erotica.** Wonderful as foreplay, reading him a hot passage that describes your wished-for activity – even changing the names to yours – can bring about immediate and sizzling success.
- **Write him a note.** Send him a card or leave a note on his pillow that titillates him with the very thing that you crave: *'Can't wait to feel your*

caress on the curve of my thigh' or *'The memory of your teeth on my neck, your throat growling with passion, is driving me mad.'*

- **Respond vociferously.** Whenever he does something good, overdo your acknowledgment. Moan, shiver, scream, pant, whisper 'Yessss,' undulate, *and* compliment him afterward. It can take him a while to get the idea.

- **Tell him you had a dream.** Confide in him that during the night, you dreamt he lifted your sweater and circled your nipple with his tongue, endlessly. It made you so excited that you woke up craving him desperately. Caress him to prove it. The next time you make love, don't be surprised if he follows your dream script to the letter.

- **Make erotic deals.** With his shivering member cradled in your hand, tell him you'll give him the hottest oral sex of his life if first he massages your G-spot until you come. Or he can have a quickie now, but you get long, luxurious bathplay later. In the art of erotic deal-making, remember that (1) you always have what he wants and (2) your negotiating power is increased if your hand, mouth, or velvety vulva is in close touch with the brainstem between his legs.

- **Use the power of orgasm.** During the ecstasy of climax, we are in a hypnotic and highly suggestible state of openness. It's then that your ideas and desires can fly directly into his subconscious and lodge there, to resurface as brilliant inspirations on his part the next time you're together. If at the moment of his orgasm, you concentrate on an image of his massaging your labial lips in the tantalizing circles you adore, you can create a self-fulfilling prophecy for future lovemaking.

synchronizing his rhythms with yours

Biologically, men come to a boil and spill over very quickly, while women simmer slowly but can stay hot for hours. How to coordinate these off-kilter rhythms?

- **Circle for forty-five minutes.** After about forty-five minutes of loveplay, both your bodies undergo a physiological shift – his insistent tension relaxes into eroticism, and your body heats up and blooms voluptuously. So try to make the initial stages of lovemaking last longer. Divert attention from his throbbing appendage by massaging his upper body, sucking his toes, or offering your succulent oyster to his lips. After about three-quarters of an hour, your rhythms will be more deeply in sync.
- **Squeeze.** Use the squeeze technique during foreplay or intercourse to postpone his moment of inevitability. This gives you a chance to catch

up and also builds him to a peak of rapture he'll want to scale again in the future.

- **Use erotic logic.** Outside of the bedroom, explain to him that the longer it takes, the hotter you get, and that with patient stalking and the bait of his long, slow kisses, he can coax your animal lust out of its cage to attack him with wild abandon.

- **Start your motor running early.** Steal time on the bus ride home or while doing the dishes to think about how his long sensitive fingers make electricity run through your veins. Simmer over your own delicate fire all day if you can. Touch yourself lovingly, admiring your soft curves and secret places, building waves of orgasmic pleasure that can wash over you almost as soon as he touches your hand.

- **Use the afterglow.** The magical moments after peak ecstasy are an ideal time to balance uneven rhythms and build deeper intimacy. To prolong and enhance your own rapture, bask in the waves of pleasure that continue after orgasm, mentally rolling them through your limbs, belly, heart, and head. And while he is rapidly drifting off to dreamland, imprint your bewitching touches on his subconscious: Keep him cozy inside you and give an occasional PC squeeze; massage or lightly scratch his back; nuzzle and lick his neck; whisper how divine he made you feel and how much you loved it when he did that teasing-withdrawing-thrusting thing. Let him doze for about ten to twenty minutes, maintaining skin contact to keep the feel of love alive. Then gently awaken him and ask what he was dreaming about. These are the moments, both of you softened and saturated with bliss, when you can shape his sexual persona to fit yours like a silky glove.

As you know by now, the trick to driving a man wild in bed is simply to trigger your own intoxicating passion first. Bold, seductive, and adventurous, you become an irresistible beacon of sensuality that guides both you and your man to discover a new intensity in yourselves and your lovemaking. By daring 'to risk your body and your blood and your mind, your known self and to become more and more the self you could never have known or expected,' you find at last your true and magnificent genius as a woman and a lover.

Appendix
Safer Sex

Unfortunately, the days of completely carefree sex are no longer with us. In today's world, part of being a superb lover means taking responsibility for protecting yourself and your partner from diseases that can be incurable or even fatal. So talk frankly with each other about any risky behaviors in your past, get tested for HIV, and use latex condoms and barriers until you're 100 percent sure of each other's sexual health and commitment to responsible sex. Remember, you can be infected with AIDS and many other serious diseases through oral sex and sex toys as well as through anal or vaginal intercourse. And even with condoms, sex that involves body fluids is not completely safe, just saf*er*. Here are some basic guidelines.

- Use only *latex* condoms and barriers – viruses can pass through rubber and lambskin but not through latex.
- Never use a condom more than once.
- *Always* have him wear a condom for vaginal or anal penetration *and* for receiving oral sex.
- To prevent vaginal infections, never allow him to move directly from anus to vagina.

- Wear a dental dam when receiving oral sex from him.
- Use latex gloves for finger penetration.
- Wash sex toys in hot soapy water after each use, and apply condoms to them for playing.
- Use only *water-based lubricants* (e.g., Astroglide) with latex – oil- or petroleum-based fluids destroy latex.
- Know that the spermicide nonoxynol-9 offers *some* extra protection from germs but practically no protection from viruses – always use condoms in addition.

If *you* apply the condom, it can become an erotic and fun part of your loveplay. See pages 78 and 88 for ideas on how to roll on latex sensually with your fingers or lips. There are also a wide variety of ribbed or flavored condoms that actually enhance sensation. I know it's not ideal, but it is *necessary.* So be smart. Be firm. Be sure. Then go ahead and drive each other wild in bed. Making love with a man you feel comfortable and safe with is the greatest aphrodisiac of all.